The
Notorious
Benedict
Arnold

A
True Story
of Adventure,
Heroism & Treachery

Steve Sheinkin

SQUARE
FISH

ROARING BROOK PRESS
New York

For Rachel
On our first date, I admitted my Arnold obsession—
and she didn't run away!

🏳
SQUARE
FISH

An Imprint of Macmillan

Library of Congress Cataloging-in-Publication Data
Sheinkin, Steve.
The notorious Benedict Arnold : a true story of adventure, heroism, and bravery /
Steve Sheinkin.
p.   cm.
ISBN 978-1-250-02460-2
1. Arnold, Benedict, 1741–1801—Juvenile literature.   2. American loyalists—
Biography—Juvenile literature.   3. Generals—United States—Biography—Juvenile
literature.   4. United States. Continental Army—Biography—Juvenile literature.
5. United States—History—Revolution, 1775–1783—Juvenile literature.   I. Title.
E278.A7S5 2010   973.3'82092—dc22   [B]   2010034797

Originally published in the United States by Flash Point/Roaring Brook Press
First Square Fish Edition: February 2012
Square Fish logo designed by Filomena Tuosto
mackids.com

7 9 10 8

AR: 7.3 / LEXILE: 990L

CONTENTS

ARNOLD COUNTRY
1741~1781

LAKE ONTARIO

New York

LAKE ERIE

Pennsylvania

Carlisle •

Lancaster •

CANADA (BRITISH)

Quebec

Saint Lawrence River

Montreal

St. Johns

Maine—part of
Massachusetts

Valcour
Island

Lake
Champlain

Fort
Ticonderoga

New Hampshire

Saratoga

Massachusetts

Boston

Massachusetts

West Point

Connecticut

New Haven

Norwich

Rhode Island

Philadelphia

New York
City

New Jersey

ATLANTIC OCEAN

SCALE of MILES

0   100   200

CLEARING IN THE WOODS
October 2, 1780

❧

It was a beautiful place to die. The sky above the woods glowed blue, and the leaves on the trees were a riot of fall colors: sunshine yellow, campfire orange, blood red.

In a grassy clearing, a small group of American soldiers quickly built a gallows. It was a simple structure, made of two tall, forked logs stuck into the ground, with a third log laid horizontally between the forks. The soldiers tied one end of a rope to the middle of the horizontal log, letting the other end hang down. There was no platform to stand on, no trapdoor to fall through— the prisoner would have to climb onto a wagon with the rope looped around his throat. Horses would jerk the wagon forward, and he would tumble off the back. The force of his falling weight should be enough to snap a man's neck.

As the soldiers worked, a crowd began to gather. Officers rode up and sat still on their horses. Soldiers and citizens from nearby towns gradually filled the clearing. By late afternoon, hundreds of people surrounded the gallows, and thousands lined the road leading to it. It was a somber crowd. People spoke in whispers, if at all.

Shortly before five o'clock, a wagon carrying a plain, pine coffin rattled along the road and into the clearing. The driver stopped his horses just beyond the gallows, with the wagon lined up under the dangling rope. The ghoulish figure of a hangman appeared, his face sloppily smeared with black axle grease to disguise his identity. He stood by the wagon and waited.

A few minutes after five, the distant sounds of a fife and drum band reached the clearing. The music grew louder, and the crowd recognized the tune—a funeral march. Soon the players came into view, stepping slowly and heavily in time with the music.

Behind the band marched the prisoner. He wore a spotless officer's uniform, his long hair pulled back and tied neatly behind his neck. When he reached the clearing he saw the gallows and stopped. The color drained from his skin. He swallowed, making a visibly painful effort to force the saliva down his throat. Then he began marching again, walking steadily toward his death.

But this is the end of the story. The story *begins* thirty-nine years earlier and 125 miles to the east, in the busy port town of Norwich, Connecticut. The story begins with Benedict Arnold.

BENEDICT ARNOLD

January 14, 1741

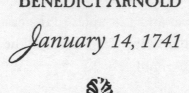

He was the sixth Benedict Arnold.

The first Benedict Arnold sailed from England to America in the early 1600s. He settled with his family in Newport, Rhode Island, became a wealthy landowner, and was elected governor of Rhode Island ten times— still a record. His son, the second Benedict Arnold, mismanaged the family's estate and lost most of the money, though he did serve several terms in the colony's House of Deputies. The third Benedict Arnold was not elected to anything, as far as we know. He inherited just enough land for a modest farm, farmed badly, apprenticed his son to a barrel maker, and died poor.

Determined to turn the family fortunes around, the fourth Benedict Arnold learned to make barrels, moved to Norwich, Connecticut, and went to work for a prosperous merchant and sea captain named Absalom King. After King died suddenly of smallpox, Arnold married King's widow, Hannah, and himself became a captain and successful merchant. Hannah gave birth to the fifth Benedict Arnold in 1738, but the child died of fever at just ten months. She had a second son on January 14, 1741. The boy was given the same name as his dead brother.

The Arnolds feared for their new baby. He was born right in the middle of one of the coldest months on record in the northeast, before or since. Early in January a mass of arctic air blew down from Canada and sat on coastal Connecticut, driving temperatures far below zero and holding them there for twenty days. Frozen snow covered fields and towns, silent roads, and abandoned wharfs. The streams froze, then the rivers, then, for the first time in local memory, shallow sections of ocean. Families huddled indoors, shivering when they stepped a few feet from the fireplace. It was a very bad time to be a newborn.

The sixth Benedict Arnold surprised everyone by surviving.

PRANKS AND PLAYS

1751–1762

Ten-year-old Benedict Arnold walked through the streets of Norwich with a sack of corn over his shoulder. He was on his way to the mill to have the corn ground into cornmeal.

When Benedict got to the mill, he saw a line of people ahead of him. This was not a boy who liked to wait. Reluctantly taking his place in line, he stood watching the rushing stream turn the mill's huge wooden waterwheel. He looked again at the people in front of him— impatient boys and chatting adults: a perfect little audience.

Without a word, Benedict dropped his sack of corn, sprinted to the bank of the stream, and leaped through the air toward the spinning waterwheel. He slammed hard into the turning wheel, but managed to grab hold of one of the wet wooden spokes. Wrapping his body around the soggy wood, he rose high in the air, then swung upside down as the wheel turned, disappearing underwater. Seconds later he burst up with the wheel, dripping and smiling.

As he rose for another spin, he turned toward the line of people outside the mill. The boys grinned with admiration; the adults were in shock. The best part: they were all looking at him.

The people of Norwich soon got used to this kind of behavior. One local resident remembered young Benedict Arnold as a "daredevil." Another, an early teacher, called him "a bright boy, so full of pranks and plays."

Locals described Benedict as lean and strong, always carefully dressed in fine clothes. When not stuck in school or church, Benedict could be seen running or swimming, or sailing small boats, or jumping onto ships at the wharf and wriggling up the tallest masts just for the joy of the challenge. If the ship's captain came out to curse him, he'd dive off into the river and swim to a safe distance. He was a thrill seeker, a natural athlete, a born show-off.

When Benedict was eleven years old, his parents sent him to a respected boarding school in the nearby town of Canterbury. There his troubles began.

∽

In August 1753, Benedict opened a letter from his mother, Hannah. He was expecting routine news about his father and his three younger sisters: Hannah, Mary, and Elizabeth. Instead he read: "Deaths are multiplying all 'round us, and more daily expected, and how soon our time will come, we know not."

An epidemic of yellow fever was ripping through Norwich, and Benedict's sisters all had the telltale chills and yellow eyes. Benedict wanted to rush home to be with his family, but his mother refused to let him come—not while the deadly fever was still spreading. So he stayed at school, helplessly waiting for news.

Two weeks later his mother sent a terrifying update: "For three or four days past we looked on Mary as one just stepping off the banks of time, and to all appearances, Hannah just behind." Prepare for the worst, she told her son. "What God is about to do with us I know not," she wrote, "We have a very uncertain stay in this world."

The next letter brought more news: Hannah seemed to be out of danger, but eight-year-old Mary was dead. Soon after that, his youngest sister, Elizabeth, also died. Benedict could not come home for the funerals for fear of catching the fever.

It was at about this time that twelve-year-old Benedict's "pranks and plays" took on a different, more aggressive form. One day a barn near his schoolhouse caught fire, and Benedict and the other boys ran out to watch it burn. Their teacher arrived moments later, glanced through the small crowd, and demanded to know where Arnold had gone. The boys looked around. He had been there a moment earlier.

Then the mystery was solved—everyone looked up at the burning barn and there, on top of the slanted roof, holding out his arms for balance, was Benedict Arnold. Through black smoke and rising orange flames the boys and teacher watched Benedict walk from one end of the barn to the other. Death may have taken his sisters. Balancing on the burning roof, Benedict was fighting back, letting death know *he* would not go quietly.

The yellow fever epidemic eventually ran its course in Norwich, but the Arnold family troubles only deepened. Throughout Benedict's early childhood, the Arnolds had been among the richest families in Norwich. But that was changing. An economic slowdown in New England was killing his father's shipping business. As debts piled higher, creditors began threatening to have Captain Arnold arrested for his failure to pay. The constant stress fueled an even bigger problem: Captain Arnold's drinking. He'd always enjoyed his rum, but after watching his daughters die and his business collapse, he started drinking more frequently, more heavily.

"Your father is in a poor state of health," Benedict's mother wrote to the boy, disguising the true cause of the illness. She couldn't cover it up for long, though. The family's money ran out, and the Arnolds had to pull Benedict from his expensive school when he was thirteen.

Benedict may have been a troublemaker at school, but he actually enjoyed the classes and had been doing well, especially in math and Latin. He was disappointed to be forced to quit. And he was embarrassed to come home so suddenly, especially when he realized that everyone in town was gossiping about the fall of the once-proud Arnold family.

The angry teenager's response was to push his public stunts further and further. When Norwich celebrated the anniversary of a British victory over the hated French, Benedict got his hands on a pouch of gunpowder, dumped the powder down the barrel of a small cannon on the town green, followed it up with a lit match, and leaped backward. He yelled "Huzza!" as the cannon spit fire past his face.

Soon after that, he celebrated another local holiday by leading a group of boys down to a waterfront shop and stealing some empty barrels. The plan was to make an enormous bonfire. But the shop owner saw the theft and shouted for help. When a constable came running, the boys left the barrels behind—all the boys except Benedict, that is, who stripped off his coat and dared the big man to a fistfight. He continued challenging the constable, even as the much stronger man carried him, kicking and cursing, from the street.

Within a year of Benedict's return to Norwich, his father was finally arrested and jailed briefly for not paying his debts. The family's dreams of sending Benedict to college were abandoned.

Unable to handle both a husband incapacitated by alcohol and an increasingly wild son, Hannah arranged for the fourteen-year-old Benedict to spend the next seven years as an apprentice with Daniel Lathrop, a relative of hers who ran an apothecary shop in town.

There are only scraps of evidence from this period, and they suggest that Benedict recognized this as a valuable opportunity, and behaved well. Channeling his energy into hard work, he learned to mix medicines and run the store. The only trouble came during the French and Indian War, when Arnold, then eighteen, ran off, without permission, to join the fighting. He was training at an army camp in New York when he heard from someone who'd recently come from Norwich that his mother was very sick, possibly dying. Arnold deserted the army and raced back to his family's home. He sat by his mother's bed for days, leaving only for brief periods to hide in the attic whenever army recruiters came through town. Hannah died in August 1759.

Arnold returned to the Lathrops' shop to finish his apprenticeship. He gained the Lathrops' trust, and they began sending him on trading voyages to Canada, the Caribbean, even Great Britain.

But life in Norwich was only getting worse, as Arnold's father slipped further out of control. Church leaders threatened him. The justice of the peace issued an arrest warrant, stating: "Benedict Arnold [Senior] of Norwich was drunk in said Norwich, so that he was disabled in the use of his understanding and reason."

Night after humiliating night, the younger Arnold was sent out to search the waterfront taverns for his father. He often had to literally drag the groaning, puking, crying man through the streets to their home. Curious eyes looked out from doorways and windows. Arnold felt the eyes watching him, judging him.

⌒

The old man finally died in 1762, leaving his son with nothing but debts and a fouled family name. Benedict Arnold was just twenty-one, but his many-sided character was already well formed. He was smart, a quick learner, and a hard worker with a ferocious determination to succeed. He longed for action, craved attention, and bristled at anything he perceived as criticism or disrespect. He respected authority when it suited him, but made his own rules when he felt the situation warranted. And he had a bold recklessness, a hunger for danger that both excited people and intimidated them. He was just beginning to realize what a useful weapon this could be.

These traits made an explosive mix, more than enough fuel to power a dazzling rise—and a spectacular crash.

MAKING OF A REBEL

1762–1775

When Arnold's apprenticeship ended, the Lathrops gave him some money to help him get started on his own. Arnold sailed to London to buy goods and opened his own shop in New Haven, Connecticut. He sold books and maps, cosmetics and jewelry, and some of the medicines he'd been trained to make, including various cold cures and an aphrodisiac called "Francis' Female Elixir."

At twenty-one, Arnold was the head of his family, which included only himself and his eighteen-year-old sister, Hannah. Hannah helped run the business, taking over entirely when Arnold sailed off on long trading voyages. Arnold, in turn, took his position as head of the family seriously—perhaps too seriously. Late one night he was walking home with a friend when he saw, through the lighted living room window, Hannah

14

sitting with a French gentleman, a man Arnold had warned to stay away from his young sister.

Arnold told his friend to go to the front door and open it loudly. While the friend walked toward the door, Arnold loaded and cocked a pistol, and crouched in the shrubs beneath the window. The friend opened the front door as instructed. Thinking it was Hannah's over-protective brother, the Frenchman leaped from the couch, tripped to the window, lifted the glass, jumped out, and sprinted down the dark street. Arnold took a shot toward the bouncing figure, purposely aiming just a little high.

That was the last time anyone saw Hannah's French-man.

Over the next few years, Arnold was too focused on busi-ness to care much about politics—until politics began to threaten his business.

Soon after the French and Indian War ended in 1763, the victorious but deeply indebted British gov-ernment decided to tax the American colonists. With no representation in the British Parliament, colonists protested that Britain had no right to tax them. Along with merchants all over the Colonies, Arnold refused to pay the duties on imported goods. Instead he became a tax protester—and a smuggler. This led to an important turning point in Arnold's life.

In January 1766, a sailor named Peter Boles was seen sneaking into the customs house at the New Haven waterfront. The customs commissioner wasn't there, and Boles came back out moments later. But Arnold could guess what had just happened. Boles had meant to inform the commissioner that Arnold was importing goods without paying British taxes. He was hoping to collect a reward for turning Arnold in.

Boles, who'd been a sailor on Arnold's most recent trading trip, had some gripe against Arnold; we don't know the details. Arnold insisted that during the entire voyage Boles "was used with the greatest humanity." In any case, whatever Boles's grievance was, the sailors' unwritten code was clear: a man does not inform on his fellow sailors.

That night Arnold found Boles in Beecher's Tavern. Arnold threatened Boles, forcing him to sign a statement saying: "I justly deserve a halter for my malicious and cruel intentions. . . . I will immediately leave New Haven and never enter the same again." Then Arnold went home, satisfied.

"Near four hours after, I heard a noise in the street," Arnold later said. A group of his sailors were gathering at his front door. Boles was still in town, they told Arnold, still drinking at the same tavern.

With his men marching behind him, Arnold strode to Beecher's, kicked in the door, and dragged Boles outside and across the street to the whipping post, where, in Arnold's words, Boles "received near forty lashes with a small cord." Then Arnold's crew carried Boles to the edge of town and dumped him on the muddy road.

The upper-class folks of New Haven were already alarmed by the frequent tax protests, which they saw as disobedience to authority. When they heard that Arnold had whipped Boles in the street, they were horrified. "The growing disorder and violence and breaches of law in this town are become very threatening to the public peace," declared the *Connecticut Gazette*.

Arnold was charged with beating Boles in what his arrest warrant called "a shocking, cruel, and dangerous manner." He was tried and found guilty, but the judge fined him only fifty shillings—a token punishment. This was a town that relied on shipping and trade, and the majority of the people of New Haven were behind Arnold. The Boles incident made Arnold a leader of the rising opposition to British taxes—and a local celebrity.

෧

A friend described Benedict Arnold as "something below the middle height, well formed, muscular, and capable of great endurance."

"He was dark skinned," said another man, "with black hair, and middling height."

A third description: "He was well formed, very stoutly built."

People spoke of his large nose and intense, glowing gray eyes. They said he was a lover of racing, horseback riding, fencing, shooting, boxing—any kind of competition. He was known for his ability to jump over a wagon, never touching hand or foot to the wood. His showy ice-skating style was legendary as well. "The most accomplished and graceful skater I have ever seen," said one man.

In February 1767, he married a young woman named Margaret Mansfield, whom locals described as pretty and very shy. He was twenty-six, she was twenty-two.

In the five years after their marriage, Margaret gave birth to three sons: Benedict, Richard, and Henry. Other than that, we know very little about their relationship, but tension comes through clearly in letters Arnold wrote home during his long trading trips. "I have now been in the West Indies seven weeks and not heard one syllable from you since I left home," wrote Arnold in one letter.

This became a common theme. "I am now under the greatest anxiety and suspense," he wrote to his wife while off on another voyage, "not knowing whether I write to the dead or the living, not having heard the least syllable from you these last four months."

During another long absence, someone in New Haven spread the story that Arnold was having an affair with a woman in the Caribbean. Margaret was shaken, and when Arnold got home, he was told to sleep on a couch. He furiously denied the charge and spent months collecting sworn testimony from fellow ship captains, who testified to Arnold's good behavior.

Another swirling rumor was that Arnold fought duels in the Caribbean, and this we know is true.

There may have been several, but one duel is well documented. Arnold was docked in the Bay of Honduras, doing some last-minute paperwork before leaving for home, when a sailor from a British ship rowed up. The man handed Arnold a dinner invitation from Captain Croskie, the sailor's captain.

Arnold was too busy to go to the dinner, but he forgot to send Croskie a formal reply, which was a serious breach of etiquette. The next morning he rowed over to Croskie's ship to apologize. As Arnold opened his mouth to speak, the hungover British captain snapped, "You are a damned Yankee, destitute of good manners or those of a gentleman!"

Arnold said nothing. He just took off a glove and handed it to Croskie—the acknowledged challenge to a duel.

The next morning Arnold and Croskie, along with their seconds and a surgeon, met on the beach of a nearby island. The opponents were handed loaded pistols and stood about thirty feet apart. Croskie, as the challenged party, had the right to fire first. Arnold stood perfectly still on the hot sand. Croskie lifted his gun, fired, and missed. Arnold then fired and grazed Croskie's arm. The surgeon bandaged the slight wound, and the men returned to their positions.

It was Croskie's turn to fire next. Arnold looked at the British captain and said, "I give you notice, if you miss this time, I shall kill you."

Red-faced, sweating, bleeding, Croskie decided he had not been insulted by Arnold after all. He apologized for any offense he may have given and reached out his hand toward Arnold. The men shook hands, got into a boat, and rowed away from the island, the best of friends.

That was how Benedict Arnold lived his life. There were long periods of hard work, occasionally interrupted by explosions of temper. The work part was paying off—his business was thriving. In 1770 he started building his dream home, a mansion on the New Haven waterfront.

That same year British soldiers in Boston fired into a crowd of tax protestors, killing four. Arnold expressed shock and anger, both at the Boston Massacre itself, and at the fact that his countrymen didn't respond by rioting in the streets. "Good God!" he cried. "Are the Americans all asleep and calmly giving up their glorious liberties?"

The British continued trying to tax the colonists, and colonists continued resisting. In 1773 the members of a secret organization called the Sons of Liberty protested British taxes by disguising themselves as Indians and dumping three hundred crates of British tea into Boston Harbor. Arnold heartily approved of the Boston Tea Party. When he heard that a local Loyalist, Reverend Samuel Peters, had spoken out against the Tea Party and rowdy Patriots in general, Arnold led a group of Sons of Liberty to the New Haven house where Peters was holed up.

"Bring an axe, and split down the gate!" Arnold shouted.

Peters hunched inside, clutching a gun. "Arnold," he responded, "so sure as you split the gate, I will blow your brains out."

Arnold stepped away from the house. Someone in the mob cried, "Coward!"

"I am no coward," Arnold said. "But I have no wish for death at present."

As Britain clamped down harder on the Colonies, colonial towns formed militias and prepared to fight. Arnold was one of the first to volunteer in New Haven. When militia members met to elect their leader in early 1775, Arnold was the man they chose.

Benedict Arnold had risen quickly since the end of his apprenticeship—from a teenager dusting bottles and mixing powders, to a wealthy merchant, owner of a showy home, and leader of the local Patriots.

It was not nearly enough for him. Everyone still remembered the long decline of Arnold's family, still talked about his father's public drunkenness, his own wild youth. This is what made the coming war with Britain so important to Arnold. Yes, he believed in the cause of American independence, but there was much more to it.

War would be a heaven-sent chance to wipe out the marks against him, to soar up and over everyone who'd ever dared to judge him.

He could do more than just restore the Arnold name— he could make it immortal.

ARNOLD'S WAR
April 19–May 9, 1775

The war Arnold was hoping for began on April 19, 1775, when nearly a thousand British soldiers marched out of Boston toward Lexington and Concord. They had orders to seize supplies from colonial militias, but armed Americans blocked the road, sparking a long day of frantic fighting. The British made it back to Boston that night, but not before three hundred of them were killed or wounded. Express riders sped through the Colonies with the shocking news.

Two days later, Benedict Arnold joined the American Revolution. He stepped out of the front door of his waterfront home, looking sharp in his militia officer's uniform: a bright scarlet coat, white pants and stockings, black boots, and a sword at his side. Behind him came his wife and their three sons, ages seven, six, and three.

The family walked down the steps and into the street. As the Arnolds strode through town, militia members scrambled out of nearby houses and fell in behind them. There were ten, then twenty, then nearly sixty. Hundreds of women and children and old men rushed out to join the march.

When this odd parade reached the town green, family members stood to the side as Arnold formed his militiamen into neat rows. He led them across the green to Hunt's Tavern, placing the men in an arcing line before the building.

Through the tavern windows, New Haven's town leaders could be seen peeking out, looking concerned. Moments later the tavern door opened. Out came sixty-five-year-old David Wooster.

Arnold got right to the point: he was about to lead the New Haven militia on a march toward Boston, and his men needed weapons and gunpowder. He held out his hand and demanded the keys to the town's powder house.

"This is Colony property," Wooster pointed out.

Arnold agreed that it was Colony property. He demanded that Wooster hand it over.

Wooster shook his head. "We cannot give it up without regular orders from those in authority."

"Regular orders be damned!" Arnold shouted.

Wooster nodded, buying time. Then, motioning toward the tavern, he began to explain that he and the other town leaders were this very moment discussing the recent fighting in Lexington and Concord, and had not yet decided whether it would be prudent to send the town's militia to Massachu—

"Our friends and neighbors are being mowed down by the Redcoats!" Arnold cut in. "Give us powder or we will take it!"

Wooster opened his mouth to try again. He was too slow.

"None but Almighty God shall prevent my marching!" barked Arnold. And to accentuate the point, he ordered his men to kick in the powder house door.

That did the trick—Wooster went to get the keys.

Arnold and his men arrived in Cambridge, across the river from British-held Boston, on April 30. The American camp was a mess—ten thousand militiamen living in tents, their trash piling up and rotting. The Americans had Boston surrounded, totally bottled up. But they couldn't hope to take the well-defended city without some cannon, and they had none.

Arnold had a solution. Trading trips had taken him all over the northern Colonies, and he'd seen Fort Ticonderoga, a British fort on Lake Champlain in northern New York. A few dozen British soldiers stood guard. And the fort had nearly a hundred cannon—there for the taking.

Arnold went directly to the Massachusetts Committee of Safety, the closest thing to a government in the chaotic American camp. "I have certain information that there are at Ticonderoga eighty pieces of heavy cannon," he told colonial leaders. "The fort is in ruinous condition, and has not more than fifty men at the most." He added, "The place could not hold out an hour against a vigorous onset."

The Massachusetts men were impressed. They declared him a colonel; gave him some money, horses, and supplies; and sent him north on what they referred to as "a secret service."

Arnold had no soldiers with him—the New Haven militia stayed behind to help blockade Boston. He was supposed to recruit new fighters as he traveled. "Send forward as many men to join the army here as you can possibly spare," Arnold wrote to nearby towns. "Let every man bring as much powder and ball as he can. Also a blanket."

A week earlier, Benedict Arnold had been a merchant in New Haven. Now he was about to lead the first military attack in American history.

Six days after leaving Cambridge, Arnold crossed the border into Vermont. It was then that he heard the news. He was not the only one planning to attack Fort Ticonderoga. A group of militia officers from Hartford, Connecticut, had their own secret mission going. They had several days' head start on Arnold, and, even worse, they had recruited Ethan Allen and his Green Mountain Boys to lead the strike.

Arnold knew a bit about the Boys. Led by the six-foot-six Ethan Allen, the Boys were in a never-ending land dispute with neighboring New Yorkers. Allen had recently caught a pair of New York deputy sheriffs nosing around land he considered his. He grabbed the men, dragged them into a house, and tossed them in separate rooms. Then he went outside, to a tree he knew both men could see, and hung a realistic-looking straw man from a limb. Each New Yorker watched in horror, thinking the other was down there twisting at the end of a rope. Allen roared with laughter as first one deputy, then the second ran howling from the house, practically crashing into each other as they sprinted back toward New York.

It was the kind of stunt that Arnold could normally appreciate, but not as he and Allen sped toward the same goal.

It was well after dark when Arnold jumped off his horse outside Remington's Tavern in Castleton, Vermont. Inside was a small army of Green Mountain Boys.

Standing outside the tavern, Arnold reached into his pocket and pulled out the paper with his orders from the Massachusetts committee. This was his idea, his mission. Here was the paper to prove it. As he walked up to the tavern door, he could hear men inside shouting in drunken voices, laughing and singing. He could smell the sour stink of booze-soaked floors. Arnold hated that smell, and he had reason to hate it.

He pushed open the door and stepped inside.

The place went silent. Big men sat at long tables, staring at the stranger, who just stood there in the doorway, stiff and cocky in his scarlet jacket.

Then someone screamed: "A Redcoat!"

The men tripped over each other, cursing and stumbling toward the corners of the barroom, where their muskets were stacked.

Surrounded by weapons, the uniformed intruder held up his paper and calmly explained that he was not a British officer. He was Colonel Benedict Arnold of Connecticut. The leaders of Massachusetts had entrusted him with the mission of capturing Fort Ticonderoga. He explained that *only he* had official authority to lead the operation, and that other groups had, as he put it, "no proper orders." Then, gesturing around the room as he spoke, Arnold invited everyone in the bar to join the attack—under his command.

Arnold was met with another silence.

This one was cracked open by an explosion of laughter. The Boys slapped each other on the back, laughing so hard they gagged and cried. Some fell to the floor, others jumped onto tables and started dancing and singing.

Arnold waited, struggling to keep cool, still holding up his official orders.

A few of the Boys soon calmed down enough to explain the facts to their guest—Green Mountain Boys always elected their own officers. They served under Ethan Allen, or no one. Allen was already twenty miles north, preparing the attack on Fort Ticonderoga.

Arnold left the tavern, grabbed a few hours sleep on the ground, and then rode north to find Ethan Allen.

ACROSS THE LAKE

May 10–May 15, 1775

❧

The next day, in an open field sloping down to Lake Champlain, Benedict Arnold and Ethan Allen stood face-to-face. Arnold had to tilt his head up; he was almost a foot shorter than the burly Allen.

More than two hundred heavily armed Green Mountain Boys looked on angrily. This didn't stop Arnold from once more producing his official orders and demanding command of the attack on Fort Ticonderoga.

After staring down the visitor for a minute, Allen turned to his Boys and asked, "What shall I do with the damned rascal—put him under guard?"

Some said yes, arrest the rascal! But one of Allen's officers pointed out that Arnold actually did have official-looking orders. "Better go side by side," he said—share command, in other words.

When many of the Boys grumbled, Allen told them, "Your pay will be the same if he does command."

"Damn the pay!" they shouted.

"We won't be commanded by any others but those we engaged with!"

This went on for a while, with the Boys cursing, waving guns and axes. Arnold just stood there. Finally, Allen proposed a compromise: he and Arnold would march together at the head of the attack. Arnold agreed.

Allen sent a crew of men off to steal a boat from a Loyalist who lived on the lake. The attack would begin as soon the boat arrived.

That night Arnold walked down to the water to wait. Out there, across a mile of dark water, stood Fort Ticonderoga. Arnold crouched on thick thighs, listening for the splash of oars, hearing nothing but tiny waves lapping at the rocky beach.

It was 3:00 a.m. and drizzling when Allen's men finally rowed their stolen boat to the beach. As the exhausted raiders jumped out of the boat, Arnold, Allen, and forty fresh Green Mountain Boys crowded in and quickly crossed the choppy lake. Most of the men hopped off on the New York shore, while a few went back to pick up another load of Boys.

"I landed eighty-three men," Ethan Allen said. There was no time to wait for more—the sky above the Green Mountains was already lightening to yellowish gray. "I found myself under the necessity to attack the fort."

The small force crept toward the walls of Ticonderoga. Just one British soldier sat outside the gate. He appeared to be asleep. At a signal from Allen, the men began to run. Arnold and Allen led the charge, and Arnold quickly realized, much to his delight, that he was the faster man. By the time they reached the gate, Arnold was five yards ahead of the pack.

"Hallooo, Hallooo!" shouted the startled British soldier as the Americans approached. He lifted his gun and pulled the trigger—it misfired. He threw the thing down and ran through the open gate into the fort, still shouting, "Hallooo, Hallooo!"

A second British guard stepped forward and blasted a shot toward Arnold and Allen, missing both.

"My first thought was to kill him with my sword," Allen said. But as he brought the weapon down he changed his mind, turning the blade slightly, giving the guard what Allen called "a slight cut on the side of the head." It was plenty. The man dropped his gun and surrendered.

The Boys shouted and whooped as they poured into the fort.

Inside the fort, a British lieutenant named Jocelyn Feltham sat up suddenly in bed. He kicked off his blanket and ran, stark naked, down the hall to the door of the fort's commander, Captain William Delaplace. He pounded a few times, but the captain went on snoring. All around, the sounds of the attackers were getting louder: boots kicking wooden doors, shouted demands for surrender.

Feltham ran back to his room, threw on a coat, and was lifting a leg into his pants when someone outside his door started roaring: "Come out of there! Come out, you damned old rat!"

Pants still in hand, Feltham opened the door. There stood Ethan Allen, waving his sword, shouting: "Come out this instant, you damned skunk, or I'll sacrifice the whole garrison!" Next to Allen stood Benedict Arnold, looking irritated.

"I endeavored to make them hear me," Feltham said, "but it was impossible."

"I must have immediate possession of the fort and all the effects of George III!" bellowed Allen.

Feltham, playing it as cool as a man can while naked

from the waist down, asked, "By what authority do you demand it?"

Allen shouted, "In the name of the Great Jehovah and the Continental Congress!"

Feltham looked puzzled.

"He began to speak again," Allen remembered, "but I interrupted him, and, with my drawn sword over his head, again demanded an immediate surrender of the garrison."

"Give up your arms and you'll be treated like gentlemen," Arnold added in a calmer tone.

At this point, Captain Delaplace finally woke up. He stepped into the hall, surveyed the scene, and stammered, "Damn you, what . . . what . . . What does this mean?"

Fort Ticonderoga fell to the Americans in less than ten minutes. All forty-four British soldiers were taken prisoner, along with twenty-four women and children.

The Green Mountain Boys found ninety gallons of rum in the supply room and decided to drink it all. That's when things got really wild. The Boys rifled through the rooms, grabbing anything that looked interesting. One guy put a woman's bonnet on his head and did a hilarious dance.

Benedict Arnold was not amused. "There is here at present near one hundred men," he reported to the Massachusetts Committee of Safety, "who are in the greatest confusion and anarchy, destroying and plundering private property, committing every enormity, and paying no attention to public service."

"Colonel Allen is a proper man to head his own wild people," added Arnold, "but entirely unacquainted with military service." Technically, Arnold didn't know much about military service, either. But he knew that there was a right and wrong way to capture a fort.

Arnold ran up and down the halls, quoting military law about respecting the property of prisoners. When he saw a man running off with a sewing table, he yanked it away and handed it back to the woman who owned it.

The Boys had found Arnold annoying before the attack; now he was ruining their well-earned party. At least twice that day men fired shots in Arnold's direction. One of the Boys even lifted his musket, placed the barrel against Arnold's chest, and promised to blow a hole unless Arnold admitted that Ethan Allen had sole command of Fort Ticonderoga.

Arnold explained, as he had many times already, that he had official orders from Massachusetts to lead the attack.

Disappointed, and slightly intimidated, the man lowered his gun.

"The power is now taken out of my hands, and I am not consulted, nor have I voice in any matters," Arnold reported. "As I am the only person who has been legally authorized to take possession of this place, I am determined to insist on my right, and I think it my duty to remain here against all opposition, until I have further orders."

There were no further orders. Leaders from Massachusetts and Connecticut had independently decided to take Fort Ti, but neither colony really wanted to be in charge of it. Down in Philadelphia, the Continental Congress had just begun meeting. Members needed time to talk things over, many being far from convinced the American Colonies should fight a war with mighty Great Britain.

But Benedict Arnold was already at war with mighty Great Britain. He made a careful inspection of Fort Ticonderoga, as well as the crumbling British fort at Crown Point, ten miles to the north. And over the next few days things began breaking his way: many of Allen's men left the fort to head back to their farms, while Arnold's own recruits finally began to arrive.

Arnold's men stole a small ship named *Katherine* from a Loyalist on the lake. "We immediately fixed her with four carriage guns and six swivel guns," Arnold said. He renamed the ship *Liberty*.

"I have done everything in my power, and put up with many insults to preserve the peace and serve the public," Arnold reported to Massachusetts. He waited for further orders, but heard nothing.

Benedict Arnold never could stand inaction. So he decided to invade Canada.

TROUBLE AT FORT TI

May 18–June 19, 1775

❧

It was not quite as crazy as it sounds.

Arnold had orders to seize and hold the British forts at the southern end of Lake Champlain. He'd taken the forts, but he didn't really control them. The British still held Fort St. John's, across the border in the British colony of Canada, 120 miles to the north. At that fort was the warship *George*, by far the biggest boat on the lake. With the *George*, the British could sail south any time they chose and blast the Americans out of Crown Point and Fort Ticonderoga. So the Americans didn't really *control* the lake—not unless they could capture that warship.

The fact that no one had told Arnold to lead the first foreign invasion in American history meant nothing to him. It was the right strategic move, and he made it.

∽

Arnold picked thirty-five men for the mission, none of them Green Mountain Boys. They sailed north on the *Liberty*, reaching the northern tip of Lake Champlain by the night of May 18. Fifteen men stayed with the ship, while Arnold and the others hopped into two long canoes and rowed up the Richelieu River toward the British fort.

"After rowing hard all night we arrived within half a mile of the place at sunrise," said Eleazer Oswald, a young member of the strike force. Arnold sent a man forward to do some quick scouting. The rest of the force waited in a weedy creek, swatting mosquitoes.

"The man returning," Oswald reported, "informed us they were unapprised of our coming, though they had heard of the taking of Ticonderoga and Crown Point." The scout also reported that a major British force was on its way with orders to retake the lake. "We directly pushed for shore," said Oswald.

At six o'clock that morning Arnold's men paddled their canoes right up to the level ground in front of St. John's, where Arnold jumped out and led the charge. Caught unprepared, the sleepy British soldiers couldn't recover. "I surprised and took prisoners, a sergeant, and his party of twelve men," Arnold reported.

The attack force then moved on to the real prize—the

STEVE SHEINKIN

warship *George*. Arnold and his men leaped onto the ship and spread out, banging gun butts on cabin doors to wake the crew. They captured the *George* without firing a shot.

The men raced to load the *George* with crates of food, barrels of gunpowder, and cannon from the fort. They quickly set fire to the small British boats they couldn't take, then climbed onto the warship and pushed out into the river's south-flowing current.

"Just at the completion of our business, a fine gale arose from the north!" said Oswald. It was a lucky wind, speeding them back to American territory. "We directly hoisted sail and returned in triumph."

Arnold and his men spent the next couple of weeks digging out the cannon at Ticonderoga and Crown Point. He soon had more than a hundred big guns ready to roll south.

But Congress wasn't ready for them. The attack on Fort Ticonderoga, and now Arnold's lightning raid at St. John's—all of this was making Congress very nervous. The Americans didn't even have an official army yet. Unsure of how to proceed, members of Congress sent no clear orders about what should be done at the forts—or who was supposed to be in charge.

At this point, Arnold was faced with two things that would torment him over and over: free time and politics. He'd been busy his entire life, furiously working his way up from lowly apprentice to wealthy merchant. When he had free time on his hands he grew restless, frustrated, irritated. And Arnold had no gift for politics, the art of promoting his own image and gently persuading others to take his side. He was brash, bossy, and unable to see other people's point of view.

Ethan Allen, on the other hand, was a master of spin. Describing his capture of Fort Ti, he even made getting drunk sound gallant, writing that he and his fellow conquerors "tossed about the flowing bowl, and wished success to Congress, and the liberty and freedom of America." Allen also sent friends to Congress with his version of the action, which was basically that Allen and the Green Mountain Boys were heroes, while Arnold tagged along and drove everyone crazy.

Arnold began to worry that his hard work was going unappreciated, that his reputation was being trashed. Nothing was more certain to light the fuse of his fury.

One morning in June, Arnold was patrolling the lake on the *Enterprise*, the new name he'd given to the ship he captured at St. John's. When he saw Ethan Allen's boat sailing past Crown Point, Arnold had his soldiers stop the boat and demand a pass. This was Arnold's right as commander—a position Allen claimed for himself, of course.

Moments later one of Allen's officers, James Easton, climbed onto the *Enterprise*, pushed past the guard outside Arnold's cabin, and entered the room yelling.

Arnold stood up, lifted the butt end of his sword, and brought it down on Easton's skull. As Arnold described it: "I took the liberty of breaking his head."

Easton was knocked to his knees, glassy eyed and wobbly. Arnold gestured to the pistol in Easton's belt. Draw, he demanded, and we'll duel it out here and now.

Easton was too stunned to respond.

"On refusing to draw like a gentleman," Arnold said, "I kicked him very heartily and ordered him from the Point immediately."

An officer would certainly be kicked out of any regular army for such an outburst. But there was no Continental Army yet; no one was in charge. And so Arnold wasn't punished. He just solidified his reputation as a man slightly out of control.

On June 22 a delegation of leaders from Massachusetts came to the forts to look things over. They told Arnold to turn command of his men over to the newly arrived, and much calmer, Colonel Benjamin Hinman.

Furious at what he considered a personal affront, Arnold was heard to mumble that he'd "be second in command to no person whatsoever." He went to his ship and packed up to leave.

Just a few days later, while passing through Albany, New York, he got a message from home: his wife Margaret was dead. The doctor could find no cause.

Arnold had been craving the comfort of family. "But, oh, alas," he wrote to his sister, "how is the scene changed, every recollection of past happiness heightens my present grief."

Arnold hurried home to bury his wife. She was just thirty years old.

Enter André

June 1775

❦

Just as Benedict Arnold was leaving the Lake Champlain region, a young British officer named John André was arriving.

André was among the British soldiers sent to hold St. John's after Arnold's raid. He was assigned to patrol the Richelieu River and surrounding woods, beating back the American scouts who were constantly nosing around. "We begin to have some notion of the forces of our enemy," André wrote, "and I am happy to say that they do not appear in a very formidable light."

John André was twenty-five years old. "Well made," a friend said, "rather slender, about five feet nine inches high, and remarkably active. His complexion was dark." He had black hair and dark eyes with long lashes.

People described his face as delicate, boyish, and striking. "He was the handsomest man I ever laid eyes on," one American soldier later said. André was a talented artist and poet, and had a gift for languages, speaking fluent French, German, and Italian.

At the age of seventeen, he'd gone to work for his father's business in London, where they tried to make him a bookkeeper. He spent endless days hunched over a desk, adding figures, dreaming of something more glamorous. The one highlight was a girl named Honora. He asked her to marry him, and she agreed; but her family resisted—André had a little money, but hardly enough to support her as a gentlewoman. André tried to turn his attention back to business. He just couldn't take it. When he was twenty-one he quit and joined the army.

A few years later André was sent to the city of Quebec, Canada, where army life consisted mainly of playing his flute, making sketches of fellow officers, and going to dinner parties. Sometimes he'd brave the Canadian winter to take ladies out for sleigh rides. "I every now and then make parties into the country," he wrote to a friend. "We dine, dance, toss pancakes, make a noise, and return."

Less fun were the occasional training marches, which involved camping in what André called "the wilderness"—that is to say, outside. "The amusements of the day are to be hunting upon snowshoes or large rackets tied to one's feet," he complained. "In short we are to take humanity a peg lower."

Then the American Revolution began, leading to the American attack on Britain's Lake Champlain forts. André left the good life in Quebec and moved into the crowded fort at St. John's, where once a day he helped patrol the woods for Americans. "I had this duty yesterday," André wrote home, "and though I am not particularly keen after the pleasure of being shot at, had almost as leave have met the Yankees as been baked in the sun for the mosquitoes' dinner."

John André had been in the British army for four years. He was not sure he liked it.

A RISKY PROPOSITION
July 1–September 18, 1775

❧

Benedict Arnold stood in a cemetery on the town green in New Haven, looking down at his wife's fresh grave. Beside Arnold stood his sister, Hannah, and his three young sons.

As the family stared silently at the burial site, Arnold could feel his legs beginning to swell and ache. These were symptoms he knew—an attack of gout.

Arnold went home and got into bed. He'd had gout before, but never this bad. The joints of his elbows, knees, and toes ballooned, turned flaming red, and throbbed with pain. It hurt to move and it hurt to lie still. The weight of the sheet on his body was unbearable.

Arnold desperately needed to bury his mind in work and action. "An idle life under my present circumstances would be but a lingering death," he told Hannah, who stayed at the house to take care of the boys. But he was idle, stuck flat on his back.

From his bed, Arnold could see out the window down to the water of Long Island Sound, to the dock where his trading ships were tied up. They were idle, too. With the war brewing it was too dangerous to send unarmed ships to Canada or the Caribbean.

He could turn his head and see his wardrobe full of fine clothes, and next to it the smaller built-in closet of his own design, the one just for his huge collection of shoes. Everything in the house had been built under his direction—the marble fireplaces, the wine cellar, the porch and carved pillars out front, the stables and coach house, the gardens and fruit trees, and graveled walkways winding down to the water. The place was costing him a fortune, but it was all part of his mission to revive the Arnold name.

He needed all of it. He needed all of it, and more.

Two weeks passed and Arnold's gout still lingered. Meanwhile, the war went on without him.

The latest news from Philadelphia was that Congress had formed a Continental Army and named George Washington as its commander. Arnold knew that

Washington must be considering an invasion of Canada—if the Americans could take Canada, the British would lose its base for attacks on the Colonies. Arnold asked Hannah to bring him his maps, and he propped himself up on pillows and studied routes to Canada. He studied obvious routes and routes no one ever thought about. He had an idea.

By the end of July, Arnold was finally well enough to get back to work. He packed quickly, asked Hannah to take care of his sons, and rode off to Cambridge to meet with George Washington.

Washington was in trouble already. Just one look at the chaotic mess that was the Continental Army, and he'd begun having second thoughts about agreeing to take command.

"I daresay the men would fight very well, if properly officered," he confided to a friend, "although they are an exceedingly dirty and nasty people." The quote leaked to the press and turned up in newspapers. Washington apologized, but it was a bad beginning.

"Six-feet-two inches in his stockings and weighing a hundred seventy-five pounds," was how a fellow officer described the general. "His frame is well padded with large muscles, indicating his great strength." He had enormous feet and hands, broad shoulders, and was, according to the officer, a bit "broad across the hips."

Washington was forty-three years old, his face lightly pock-marked from a teenage bout with smallpox. We think of that famous face as stiff and emotionless, as it appears on the dollar bill, but that's not quite right according to people who knew him. He appeared calm, yes, but if you looked closely you could see he was fighting back a storm. As one friend put it, "All his features were indicative of the strongest passions."

On August 15 one of Washington's aides came into his office and told him Benedict Arnold was outside. Washington knew about Arnold's attack on Fort Ticonderoga and the raid into Canada. He knew Arnold's reputation: bright, decisive, natural leader, violent temper. He'd hear the man out.

We don't know exactly what was said at their first meeting, but we can piece together the main events. Arnold brought up the subject of an invasion of Canada. Canada is a huge place, but what mattered to the Americans was the St. Lawrence River, and specifically two cities on the river: Montreal and Quebec. If the Americans could snatch those cities, they could control the river. If they could control the river, Britain would lose its best route for attacking the northern Colonies.

Washington confirmed Arnold's deduction—the Continental Army was planning to invade Canada. A branch of the army known as the Northern Army, under the command of Philip Schuyler, a New York general, was already gearing up to lead the attack. The Northern Army would sail north on Lake Champlain into Canada, seize the British fort at St. John's, and then push up to the St. Lawrence River and Montreal.

This gave Arnold an opening to present his idea. While the main army attacked Montreal, Arnold suggested, a second, smaller force could go for Quebec. The key would be the element of surprise. If an army could march through the Maine wilderness, up and over the mountains into Canada, it could arrive at Quebec before the British had time to turn around. There was a route, Arnold explained, once used by Indians traveling in small groups. There were no accurate maps of the route, no known measurements of distances, elevations. One thing was certain, it would require traveling hundreds of miles up rocky rivers, through roadless forests and swamps. It was a journey that no one would expect an entire army to be able to complete, which is exactly why it might succeed.

It was a bold and risky proposition. Washington liked it.

Five days later, Arnold and Washington mounted their horses while the army lined up for a review. "It was in the gray of the morning," remembered an army chaplain. "With one continued roll of drums the general-in-chief with his staff passed along the whole line—regiment after regiment."

Washington told the men that Benedict Arnold, a newly appointed colonel in the Continental Army, was looking for a thousand volunteers for a secret mission. It would be very dangerous. No one was ordered to participate.

One of Washington's staff members then called out, "Volunteers step one step in advance!" More than five thousand men stepped forward. Some liked the sound of a secret mission, others just wanted out of the filthy, boring camp.

Arnold rode along the lines, asking volunteers two questions: Do you know how to live in the woods? Do you know how to handle small boats?

Nearly all of the men said yes to both, which must have made Arnold suspicious. He picked 1,050 soldiers, focusing on strong-looking types in their teens and twenties.

One exception to the under-thirty rule was Daniel Morgan, leader of a group of volunteers from the woods of Virginia. Dressed in leather leggings and loose hunting shirts, Morgan's riflemen could kill a man from 250 yards—the British named them "widow-makers." While serving with the British in the French and Indian War nineteen years earlier, Morgan had annoyed a British officer, who responded by slapping Morgan with the flat side of his sword. Morgan turned and decked the officer, for which he was sentenced to receive 500 lashes, enough to kill a good-sized bear. He stood, teeth clenched, while they slashed his back into strips of pulpy flesh. He later joked that they'd miscounted and lashed him only 499 times. Morgan was now thirty-nine, tall and strong, with a badly scarred back and a desire to kill Redcoats.

Washington reported to Congress, "I have detached Colonel Arnold with 1,000 men to penetrate into Canada by way of Kennebec River and if possible to make himself master of Quebec." To Arnold, he said, "You are entrusted with a command of the utmost consequence to the liberties of America."

Arnold sent ahead to a boat maker in Maine, ordering two hundred bateaux—flat-bottomed boats that could haul heavy supplies and navigate shallow rivers. Then he led his army north by land to the port town of Newburyport, Massachusetts, where the men spent several days collecting supplies and loading borrowed fishing boats they would sail to Maine.

When everything was ready, cheering crowds lined the road as Arnold's men marched to the wharf. A young soldier named Abner Stocking smiled at the scene. "They probably thought we had many hardships to encounter," he said, "and many of us should never return to our parents and families."

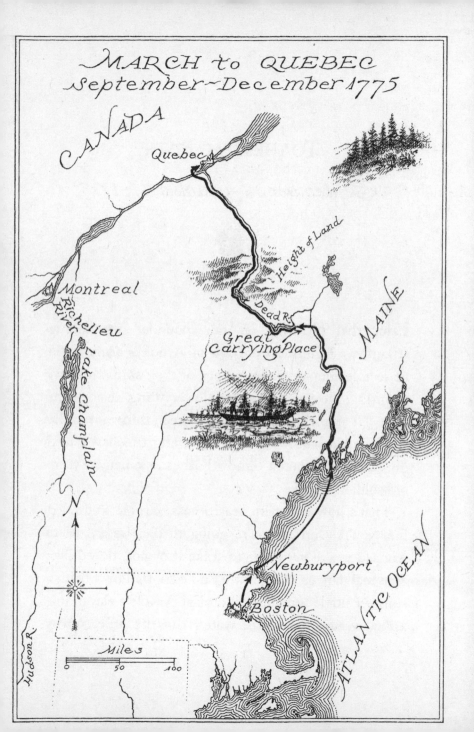

MARCH to QUEBEC
September~December 1775

To the Dead River
September 18–October 17, 1775

Later that morning, as rain pounded the rolling Atlantic, a significant portion of Arnold's army could be seen leaning over the railings of their ships violently vomiting, heaving long after everything inside was gone. "It seemed to me that had I been thrown into the sea I should hardly have made an effort to have saved myself," remembered Simon Forbes, a nineteen-year-old soldier.

That's how it is with seasickness, Arnold knew. At first you're worried you're going to die. Later, you're worried you're *not* going to. Like it or not, they'd live. The real danger was that they'd be spotted by a British ship—a single warship could blast Arnold's eleven unarmed vessels out of the water. But the little convoy made it undetected to the mouth of the Kennebec River and sailed up the river and out of sight of British ships.

Once the fleet was safely on the river, Arnold got on a horse and rode ahead to the shipyard of Reuben Colburn, where the bateaux were being built. When he got there he saw rows of twelve-foot boats lined up along the river. They looked good, until he got close enough to see that they'd been made from wet, green pine planks that were already beginning to shrink and bend as they dried. Arnold grabbed the bow of a boat, tried to lift it, and almost wrenched his back—the thing weighed four hundred pounds. "I found the bateaux completed," he reported to Washington, adding the comment: "very badly built."

Was this the first recorded case of a contractor ripping off the American government? Not really. Colburn had gotten the order less than three weeks before, and had worked furiously with the best materials he could find.

On September 27 the soldiers jumped into their heavily loaded bateaux and pushed into the Kennebec River. There were 1,050 men and three women. Two of the women were soldiers' wives who had come along because they were worried about their husbands' health; the third was Jacataqua, a young Abenaki Indian beauty who'd been invited by one of Arnold's volunteers, a teenager named Aaron Burr. There was at least one dog that we know of on the journey, Captain Henry Dearborn's beloved black Newfoundland.

Arnold rode in a birchbark canoe, which was lighter and faster than the bateaux, allowing him to dart back and forth with orders and encouragement. "To Quebec and victory!" he shouted to each boat, calling the men by name as he paddled past. The men roared cheers and returned the call: "To Quebec and victory!"

The cheering didn't last. A summer drought had left the waters of the Kennebec low, with sharp rocks jutting up everywhere. Experienced men would have had a hard time steering the clunky boats against the river's obstacles and rushing current, and, as Arnold quickly realized, most of the men had no idea what they were doing.

The only way to make progress was to use long poles to push the boats forward a few feet at a time. Even this only worked when some of the men stood in the icy water—one in front of each boat, pulling it forward by a rope tied to the bow, and another in back, holding the boat so it wouldn't tip over. "The men in general, not understanding bateaux, have been obliged to wade and haul them," Arnold wrote to Washington. "You would have taken the men for amphibious animals, as they were a great part of the time underwater."

That was the easy part.

The hard part was when they came to whitewater rapids and waterfalls. Then they had to push the bateaux to the shore, unload the nearly one thousand pounds of goods on each boat, and then yank the boats out of the water. They lifted the boats—four men to a boat—turned them upside down, set them on their shoulders, and inched slowly uphill over rolling rocks and loose dirt. "Our progress under these immense burdens was indeed slow," reported a volunteer named George Morrison.

Then it was back into the river, where the boats began to leak as the green wood warped, opening gaps between the planks. "Could we have then come within reach of the villains who constructed these crazy things, they would have fully experienced the effects of our vengeance," one soldier said. Of course, it didn't help that the boats kept slamming into rocks, making the holes bigger. Soon the men were bailing constantly, scooping puddles from the bottoms of the boats. Other soldiers took turns walking alongside the boats, slipping on the slick rocks under their feet, sometimes disappearing over their heads into unseen pools. Many of the men couldn't swim and needed to be rescued. Two drowned.

On October 2 the army reached Norridgewock Falls, the last place, they were told, where they'd find houses or farms along the river. "Here we leave the English settlements," Arnold wrote in his journal. "The mountains begin to appear on each side of the river, high, and snow on the tops."

The men went to sleep in their wet uniforms, as they had every night for a week. This time they woke to find their clothing frozen stiff, an alarming reminder that it was late in the year to be starting a long journey in this northern country. Food was becoming a problem too, as the leaking boats let water into the food barrels. When the men opened a few barrels to inspect the contents, they saw their salted meat squiggling with maggots.

But this was just the beginning of the journey, and the men were hardly discouraged. When they got back in the river, Arnold paddled up and down the line of boats, cheering the men on. And when they reached yet another rocky rapid, Arnold jumped out and took a place carrying one of the heavy bateaux. "Our commander, Arnold, was a remarkable character," said John Henry, a sixteen-year-old member of the mission. "He was brave, even to temerity, and was beloved by the soldiery."

On October 10 Arnold wrote in his journal: "Arrived at the Great Carrying Place, which is very remarkable." Aptly named by the Abenaki Indians, this was the spot where, to follow the route to Quebec, the troops would have to drag their boats out of the Kennebec River and carry them thirteen miles to the Dead River. The route across the carrying place was heavily forested, dotted with three large ponds, and rose a thousand feet from the Kennebec to the Dead.

Daniel Morgan and his brawny riflemen lead the way, hacking down trees to widen the old Indian path. Other soldiers unloaded the boats, turned them bottom up, lifted them onto their shoulders, and got started. The ground looked firm, but that was deceptive. "A complete bog," was how George Morrison described the land. "We were often half-leg deep in the mud, stumbling over fallen logs, one leg sinking deeper in the mire than the other, then down goes the boat and carriers with it."

"Every step we made sunk us knee-deep in a bed of wet turf," reported John Henry. "My feet were pained and lacerated by the snags of the dead pines, a foot and more below the surface of the moss."

The heavy boats scraped and rubbed the men's shoulders, wearing through their shirts, and then their skin, until the white tips of bones poked out. When they reached the first pond, the muddy men turned back to get the massive barrels of food. "Our men are fatigued in carrying over their bateaux, provisions, etc.," Arnold wrote, "the roads being extremely bad—however their spirit and industry seems to overcome every obstacle and they appear very cheerful."

When it was finally time to sleep, the soldiers collapsed on patches of cold moss. George Morrison expected to pass out before his head hit the dirt, but was in for a bitter disappointment. "The ground was so soaked," he noted, "that the driest situation we could find was too wet to lay upon any length of time; so that we got but little rest." He and the others sat up all night, shivering around a campfire. Then they did it all again for six more days and nights.

"The army was now much fatigued," said the mission's twenty-two-year-old doctor, Isaac Senter. Knowing the men would be desperate for cool water, he warned them not to drink from the second pond along the route, noting in his journal: "Water was quite yellow."

The temptation was too great—sweat-soaked soldiers dropped to their stomachs and gulped from the stagnant pool. "No sooner had it got down than it was puked up by many of the poor fellows," Senter lamented. When they were done throwing up, the evil yellow water started coming out the other end. "Many of us were now in a sad plight with the diarrhea," said Senter. Arnold had to have a log cabin built to serve as a temporary hospital. By September 17 he reported that his force was down to "950 effectives."

For those still able to walk, it took seven trips back and forth across the Great Carrying Place to get all the boats and supplies to the Dead River. The army camped on the riverbank, resting their bruised and aching bodies, thinking about the journey still ahead. So many barrels had gotten wet that they were nearly out of food. They were still a long way from the nearest Canadian towns—French villages where the people hated the British and could be counted on to sell Arnold supplies. But Arnold guessed it would take as much as two weeks to reach these towns.

Then it started to rain.

CRITICAL AND ALARMING
October 19–October 29, 1775

❧

Arnold's men paddled easily against the kind of gentle current you'd expect from a river named Dead. But the endless rain was slowly bringing the river to life. "Prodigious fall of rain for two days past has raised the river upwards of three feet," Arnold noted on October 19.

That night the men set up camp beside the swollen river and struggled to light fires. "It was near eleven o'clock before we could dry clothes and take a little refreshment," said Arnold. "We wrapped ourselves in our blankets and slept."

The rain kept falling—it was actually the remains of a hurricane sweeping inland—raising the Dead River another nine feet after nightfall. At four in the morning Arnold's men woke suddenly to the sound of the river roaring toward them, "rushing on us like a torrent,"

Arnold said. "And before we could remove," he reported, the surging water "wet all our baggage, & forced us from our comfortable habitation."

The army huddled on a small hill, teeth chattering, dodging falling limbs that the whipping wind kept cracking off trees all around them.

When the sun finally rose, Arnold stood on his hill and looked out at a watery world. There was nothing in sight but trees sticking up from swirling black water.

"This morning presented us a very disagreeable prospect," he noted, "the country round entirely overflowed." There was absolutely no way to tell where the Dead River used to be.

Knowing the general direction he needed to follow, Arnold and his soldiers got back into their bateaux. The current was so strong now that men had to lie in the bow of each boat, grab the trunks of partially submerged trees, and pull the boat forward. When men lost their grip on the slippery bark, the boats swung sideways, sped backward, and slammed into tree trunks. Five boats broke to pieces and sank. The men in the boats were saved, but more of their scarce food was lost.

After covering just half a mile, Arnold set up camp on another little hill. The men gave this place a name that reflected their mood—Camp Disaster.

Before, they'd just been tired and in terrible pain. Now the men were genuinely scared. "I am at this time well, but in a dangerous situation," wrote a soldier named Timothy Bigelow. "We are in a wilderness nearly one hundred miles from any inhabitants."

"At this critical and alarming crisis a council was called to consider what was most prudent to be done," remembered Abner Stocking. A few men slapped together a little lean-to of logs, and Arnold and his officers hunched and crowded inside. There was a fire in the middle of the space, but all it managed to do was blind the men with smoke rising from the soggy logs.

Surrounded by bursts of coughs and sneezes, Arnold reviewed the facts: They did not know exactly where they were or how much farther they needed to go. If and when they managed to stumble out of the wilderness, it was possible the British would be there waiting to wipe them out. And they were just about out of food. The question before them was whether to go on, or to turn back while they might still have a chance to make it home alive. Arnold asked for opinions.

There was silence, except for the sizzling and popping

of wet wood, and teeth chattering. Then, one by one, the officers voted to go on.

"We could be in no worse situation if we proceeded on our route," said Henry Dearborn. Arnold nodded in agreement.

"Our march has been attended with an amazing deal of fatigue," Arnold wrote in a report to Washington. "I have been much deceived in every account of the route, which is longer and has been attended with a thousand difficulties I never apprehended." He added, "But if crowned with success, I shall think it but trifling."

Early the next morning he picked a small group of men and set off ahead of the main army on a race for the nearest Canadian towns. His hope was to send back food before it was too late. Before setting out he dashed off orders to Lt. Colonel Roger Enos, who commanded the division in the rear of the march. Enos had the army's last food reserves, and Arnold ordered him to send forward as much as he could spare. "Pray make all possible dispatch," he urged.

And Enos did make "all possible dispatch"—to save himself. He and his officers decided to turn back, taking three hundred men and the last of the food.

The remaining soldiers were shocked and furious.

"Our men made a general prayer that Col. Enos and all his men might die by the way, or meet with some disaster," said Dearborn. "And then we proceeded forward."

"We are in an absolute danger of starving," said John Topham, a young officer. The men were now boiling down their candles and eating them mixed with their last few grains of wheat. They boiled what was left of their shoes, drank the broth, and tried to chew the leather.

With this for nutrition, the army paddled up the Dead River to the Height of Land, a ridge of mountains dividing Maine and Canada. Here the men left their batcaux behind and continued on with just the supplies they could carry. "The ascent and descent of the hill was inconceivably difficult," George Morrison said. "We were very feeble from our former fatigues and short allowances of but a pint of flour per man per day for nearly two weeks past."

On the night of October 24 the rain finally stopped—turning instead to snow. Men woke up under six inches of icy powder. They brushed themselves off and continued the climb.

As they hiked up and down rugged hills, the weakened men became confused and dizzy. They saw rocks in their path, but lacked the strength and balance to avoid tripping over them. Men tried to support each other, but only ended up knocking each other down. "Whose heart would not have melted at this spectacle?" Morrison wondered.

On October 29 the men finally tumbled down the last slopes of the Height of Land. Next they needed to reach the Chaudière River, which flows north into the St. Lawrence near Quebec. Arnold had sent back a scout with directions on how to get through the swamps between this spot and the Chaudière, but the army was so spread out that most of the men missed the message.

In small groups, the men marched into the unmapped swamps. "We proceeded," said Isaac Senter, "with as little knowledge of where we were, or where we should get to, as if we had been in the unknown interior of Africa."

CITY ON A CLIFF
October 29–November 8, 1775

❧

Benedict Arnold could see that the Chaudière River had been named well. *Chaudière* is the French word for boiler or cauldron, and this river boiled and bubbled over rocks as it churned north toward Quebec.

Arnold knew it would be suicidal to put boats into a river like this without first scouting the route. He had no choice. His army was back there somewhere, and he had only a few days to save it.

Arnold and his fifteen men climbed into their bateaux and were immediately swept into the current. They made great time for an hour, before shooting into a long stretch of whitewater rapids, where the men lost control. Three of the four boats flipped, sending men and supplies tumbling downstream. Two of the flipped boats crashed into rocks and splintered, as if hit by bombs.

"Happily no lives were lost," Arnold wrote, "although six men were a long time swimming in the water and were with difficulty saved."

Arnold built a fire on shore, and as soon as the soaking men stopped shivering, he pushed the small force forward. They'd lost nearly all of their food and equipment, and were down to two bateaux, which meant some of the men would have to walk. It was a disaster—a disaster that saved their lives.

Just minutes after the remaining boats pushed back into the current, one of the men walking along the river shouted, "Falls ahead!"

Arnold and his men managed to struggle to the riverbank moments before reaching a massive waterfall. Without warning, they never would have been able to stop in time. "Had we been carried over," Arnold said, "we must inevitably have been dashed to pieces and all lost."

Back with the main army, Abner Stocking was struggling through the swamp. "After walking a few hours," he said, "we seemed to have lost all sense of feeling in our feet and ankles. As we were constantly slipping, we walked in great fear of breaking our bones or dislocating our joints. But to be disabled from walking in this situation was sure death."

At night the men climbed onto tiny islands of somewhat dry ground, where they built fires and lay down with water lapping at their heads. "Every one of us shivering from head to foot," said George Morrison, "as hungry as wolves."

By morning the surface of the swamp was frozen. The soldiers slipped back into the waist-high water, cracking the ice with each forward step. Some of the men simply could not continue. Isaac Senter watched several helpless figures slip under the floating ice. "Some of them were left," he noted, "nor were heard of afterwards."

Other men used their last burst of strength to crawl up onto islands in the swamp. Leaning on trees, they called out to passing soldiers: "Will you leave us to perish in this wilderness?"

But the men who could still walk had no choice; there was no way they could support the weight of another man. Morrison spoke for his fellow travelers when he said: "My heart was ready to burst and my eyes to overflow with tears when I witnessed distress, which I could not relieve."

Then someone shouted: "Warner is not here!"

An alarmed Jemima Warner, who had made the entire march with her husband, asked for news of him.

She was told he was last seen sitting under a tree, unable to take another step. "With tears of affection in her eyes, she ran back to her husband," said John Henry.

Abner Stocking was nearby when Jemima reached her husband. He watched the couple hugging and crying as James Warner died. Jemima Warner then stood up. "She covered him with leaves," Stocking said, "and then took his gun, and left him with a heavy heart."

The army splashed and crawled out of the swamps on November 1. They had reached the Chaudière River, which was at least on the maps—they now had about forty miles to go to reach the nearest farms.

There was just one bit of food left now—Henry Dearborn's dog. When the men came to take him, Dearborn was too tired to fight. "They ate every part of him, not excepting his entrails," Dearborn said, "and after finishing their meal, they collected the bones and carried them to be pounded up, and to make broth for another meal."

Most of the men didn't get a piece of the dog and instead made a kind of gruel of their shaving soap, candle wicks, and hair grease. Then they staggered on along the snowy ground.

The next day was worse. "When we arose this morning

many of the company were so weak that they could hardly stand on their legs," Abner Stocking reported. "When we attempted to march, we reeled about like drunken men, having been without provisions for five days."

John Henry came upon a man lying on the ground, unable lift himself. Henry could see that the man was struggling to speak, and he bent down and put his ear right on the man's trembling mouth.

Henry could just make out the whispered word, "Farewell."

On November 3 Abner Stocking began to hallucinate. He closed his blurry eyes, shook his head, and looked again. The strange vision persisted: ahead of him, walking out from a cloud of fog along the river, was a cow. Several more appeared.

George Morrison saw them, too. "At this sight we made a halt," he said, "and silently gazed upon each other as if doubting our senses."

Then the men realized what had happened—Arnold had reached the nearest town and had sent back these animals for food. Some of the soldiers who'd gone ahead with Arnold walked alongside the cattle, driving them forward. There were sheep, too, and sacks of flour.

With tears streaming down their faces, the men began calling out: "Provisions in sight!"

"A cow was immediately killed and cut open," said Stocking. "I got a little piece of the flesh, which I ate raw."

"I had the good fortune to get hold of a piece of an intestine five or six inches long," said Simon Forbes. "This I washed, threw it on the coals for a short time, and then ate it with relish."

Benedict Arnold, thin and bearded, sat by a fire in a farmhouse in the French settlement of Sartigan, writing up his notes from the journey. "We have hauled our bateaux over falls, up rapid streams, over carrying places; and marched through morasses, thick woods, and over mountains," he wrote. "Thus in about eight weeks we completed a march of near six hundred miles, not to be paralleled in history."

When his soldiers began wobbling into town, Arnold went out to greet them. The entire population of Sartigan joined him in the street.

Abner Stocking realized what a strange picture the army must have made. "Our clothes were torn in pieces by the bushes and hung in strings," he said. "Few of us had any shoes."

"The people looked upon us with amazement, and

seemed to doubt whether or not we were human be-
ings," remembered Morrison. "To see a number of fam-
ished creatures, more like ghosts than men, issuing from
a dismal wilderness, with arms in their hands, was the
most astonishing site they had ever beheld."

After a few days of rest and good food, Arnold's army
pushed on the final seventy miles to the St. Lawrence
River. From the woods on the south side of the water,
they looked across the river at a walled city on a cliff, the
strongest fortress in North America, the place they had
come for—Quebec.

PRISONER OF WAR

September–November 1775

❧

One hundred miles to the southwest, the young British officer John André was trapped in a fort.

Fort is really too generous a word for the British post at St. John's. It was a cleared field in the forest, with a few brick buildings and an old wooden barn, all surrounded by a stockade of tall logs driven into the earth. Outside the walls flowed the Richelieu River. Beyond that, the woods. Beyond that, Americans.

As Washington had planned, the main thrust of the American invasion of Canada had begun in September, with General Schuyler leading the American Army north. Then Schuyler got sick and went home, and the attack continued under General Richard Montgomery. In mid-September, as Benedict Arnold's force was beginning its march through Maine, Montgomery approached St. John's with about two thousand soldiers.

The inside of the fort got very crowded very quickly. John André was just one of more than five hundred soldiers crammed into the place. Then, as the Americans approached, in poured the frightened residents of nearby farms: men, women, children, barnyard animals. A week of rain turned the ground inside the fort to a muddy pit. Soldiers huddled in what André described as "a barrack built for twenty-five men," adding, "the men had neither bedding, straw, nor blankets."

The badly outnumbered British were at first able to hold Montgomery's men back with their cannon. But as the siege continued into October, the Americans grew bolder. "We could see the enemy dragging cannon on the other side of the river," André said. The tension inside the fort set everyone on edge. One night a guard heard a rustling noise outside the walls and demanded, "Who's there?" No one answered. The man lifted his gun and blasted into the dark woods.

"In the morning a horse was found dead," André remembered. "That was the enemy that our sentry had seen and challenged."

The threat grew more serious when American artillery

opened fire, lobbing bombs into the fort. André got his first glimpse of the horrors of war—explosions blew off arms and legs, shells ripped open the buildings, sending brick and glass spinning through the crowded space.

There was no place to hide, or even to rest. "The weather grew very cold," André said, "and, as the windows of the house were all broken, as many as could find room in the cellars slept there. The rest, unable either to get a place or to bear the heat and disagreeable smell arising from such numbers being crowded together, slept above in the cold and danger."

Bombs fell at night, too, and the fort's muddy little cemetery expanded every day. One morning André looked up and saw that the Americans had dragged their cannon to a hill above the fort. "The few corners where some little shelter from the weather was to be had were now no longer tenable," he said.

Montgomery sent in a message: surrender, or else.

The British commander, Major Preston, agreed to send someone to the American camp to talk it over. He picked John André for the job. The Americans blindfolded André and led him onto Montgomery's ship, the *Liberty*—the very ship Arnold had stolen from St. John's just months before. André was quickly convinced the British position was hopeless. He took the American surrender terms back to the fort. Preston agreed to give up.

As the British soldiers marched out of the fort in their uniforms, bands playing, they got their first good look at the enemy. André saw men in farmers' clothes of all different colors, not much more than rags in many cases. Maintaining his dignity as best he could, André gently laid his sword in front of General Montgomery.

"Brave men like you deserve an exception to the rules of war," declared the American. "Let the officers and volunteers take back their swords."

According to the surrender agreement, André was to be sent south to "Connecticut or such other province as the Honorable Congress shall direct." He was to stay there until the war ended, or until there was an exchange of prisoners.

André began his march south as a prisoner of war. He had no idea where he was headed, or for how long. Or if he'd ever return.

TO THE STORMING
November 8–December 30, 1775

❦

A messenger brought Arnold the news that St. John's had fallen. "I propose crossing the St. Lawrence as soon as possible," Arnold wrote back to Montgomery, "and, if opportunity offers, of attacking Quebec."

Arnold's men gathered about thirty canoes from nearby farmhouses and carried them to the river. But it was too windy; the waters of the St. Lawrence were too choppy to attempt a crossing. The men waited five long days for better weather. Finally, on the night of November 13, the wind let up and thick clouds covered the sky. As he looked out across the water, there was just enough light for Arnold to make out the outlines of two British warships patrolling the mile-wide river.

The men climbed into the boats and pushed off. "The night being exceeding dark, everything was conducted with the utmost secrecy, no lights, no noise," remembered Jonathan Meigs. It took three trips back and forth to get Arnold's army across. The last boats were nearing the shore below Quebec when one of the overloaded canoes cracked, dumping men into the frigid river. Archibald Steele described clinging to the side of another boat—it was too crowded to take him aboard, so soldiers sat on Steele's arms, pinning him in place as his body went numb and useless with cold.

The men dragged Steele ashore and did the only thing they could to save his life: they built a fire. The light was quickly spotted by lookouts on the British warship *Hunter*. A few of the British sailors jumped on a barge and rowed over to investigate.

The Americans saw something coming and fired at the murky shapes. Moments later they heard horrible cries of pain. The barge backed away.

Just as the sky in the east began to lighten, Arnold led about five hundred men across a snowy field toward the walls of Quebec. He had not yet decided whether to risk everything on an immediate charge. Had the British gotten word of the approach of Arnold's army? Did they have enough soldiers in the city to fight off an attack? Arnold had no way of knowing.

He decided to take a closer look. His army trudged to within a mile of the city, half a mile, a few hundred yards.

As the sun came up, Arnold got his answer. Huge crowds of people were standing on top of the walls of Quebec, looking down at the Americans. Soldiers, sailors, shopkeepers, women and children, all stared in stunned silence at what appeared to be a gathering of wild beasts in the snow below.

Arnold's men were barely more than skeletons, stick figures with long matted hair and tangled beards, covered only in strips of filthy clothes. "I thought we much resembled the animals which inhabit New Spain called the orangutan," confessed Albert Stocking.

Arnold decided to have his men give a cheer for liberty. "We gave them three huzzas," said Henry Dearborn. "They did not choose to come out to meet us."

All that came out, in fact, was a cannonball, which sailed over the heads of the Americans and plunked down in the snow. The message to Arnold was clear: if you want Quebec, come and take it.

After marching to a safe distance from the British guns, Arnold dashed off a quick note to the British commander in Quebec. A soldier named Matthias

Ogden walked toward the walls waving a white flag, holding the letter, which read, "I am ordered by the Excellency Gen. Washington to take possession of the town of Quebec. I do therefore, in the name of the United Colonies, demand immediate surrender of the town."

When Ogden got close to the walls he heard a sudden explosion and saw an eighteen-pound cannonball arcing through the blue sky, heading toward him. He brought the note back to Arnold.

There was no way Arnold could seize the city. So much gunpowder had been damaged during the march that his men were down to just five rounds each. Arnold guessed that there were about two thousand soldiers in Quebec. His only choice was to pull back and try to link up with Montgomery.

On November 19, in a snowstorm, the men began another march, this time away from the city they'd come so far to take. "Most of the soldiers were in constant misery," Arnold said, "as they were barefooted and the ground frozen and very uneven. We might have been tracked all the way by the blood from our shattered hoofs."

What really tortured Arnold was that local French settlers told him the city had been wide open a few days before. British soldiers, hearing rumors of an approaching American army, had rushed into Quebec just ahead of Arnold. But there was good news, too—the British had to abandon Montreal in order to concentrate their forces in the more easily defended city of Quebec. So Montgomery's army marched right into Montreal.

"My detachments are as ready as naked men can be to march wherever they may be required," Arnold reported to Montgomery when the two armies met.

Montgomery liked what he saw, calling Arnold "active, intelligent, and enterprising," and saying, "Col. Arnold's corps is an exceedingly fine one. There is a style of discipline among them, much superior to what I have been used to see in this campaign."

Seeing Arnold's shivering men, Montgomery handed out hundreds of warm British uniforms he'd found in Montreal. The combined forces then marched back toward Quebec, with Montgomery in command.

Deciding to try once more where Arnold had failed, Montgomery wrote out a demand for surrender and convinced an old woman who lived near the fort to carry it into the city. She made it in to see the British commander, General Guy Carleton, and held out the letter to him. Without saying a word, Carleton gestured to a soldier, who picked up the tongs from beside a roaring fire. Using the tongs, the soldier took the unopened letter from the woman's hands, carried it to the fire, and dropped it in.

A few days later Montgomery sat in a wagon, riding toward a tavern for a meeting with Arnold. Just as he arrived, a British cannonball sailed out of Quebec, screamed down toward Montgomery, and sliced off the head of one his horses. The general jumped down from the wagon and walked into the tavern.

Inside, he and Arnold talked over options. There weren't many. They didn't have enough men to cut off the city and starve it to death, and they didn't have enough firepower to blast the city with heavy guns. They could walk away, or they could attack. This was an easy choice. "To the storming we must come," said Montgomery.

Arnold agreed, but brought up one tricky point: many of the men had enlisted only until January 1, which was approaching quickly. Montgomery and Arnold formed their plan. They would wait for the next stormy night, then using the swirling snow as cover, charge the city walls.

∽

After weeks of miserable precipitation, the skies suddenly cleared. The last few nights of December were freezing but dry, brightly lit by the moon and stars.

Arnold anxiously watched the weather. So did his soldiers, though with a slightly different perspective. "The attempt to storm a place so strongly fortified, I thought was rash and imprudent," said Abner Stocking, "but did not think proper to make any objections, lest I should be considered wanting in courage."

During the afternoon of December 30, the sky turned from bright blue to a glowing metallic gray. Flurries started, thickening to heavy snow soon after dark. Soldiers shouted the orders from tent to tent: "Be ready at twelve!"

BATTLE FOR QUEBEC
December 31, 1775

"The storm was outrageous," said John Henry, "the cold wind extremely biting."

With snow blowing sideways into their eyes, soldiers gathered for the attack. Many of Arnold's men were wearing British uniforms taken from Montreal, so, to distinguish themselves from the enemy, they stuck pieces of paper in their hats. On the papers they wrote, "Liberty or Death."

The plan was to simultaneously attack Quebec at different points along the walls of what locals called the "lower town"—the section near the St. Lawrence River. Arnold and Montgomery would each lead one of the charges. Once inside, they would meet up and slash their way through the city. At the same time, smaller crews would drag artillery up to the walls and blast away, hopefully creating panic and confusion, and the illusion of an attack much bigger than the one the Americans could deliver.

At 4:00 a.m. the soldiers tucked their guns into their coats to keep them dry. Some of the men lifted scaling ladders. They moved toward the city walls.

The British were expecting them. "We were all alarmed at our pickets with the report of an attack being made by the enemy," one British officer recalled. "The alarm bell of the cathedral rung, and all the drums beat to arms."

"Turn out! Turn out!" shouted voices from house to house.

American bombs started falling, smashing into streets and houses. "They sent in a number of shells," said a soldier, "which burst in all directions with a great crash, and served to increase the alarm."

"Turn out! Turn out!"

"Men of New York, you will not fear to follow where your general leads," shouted Montgomery to his men. "Come on, my brave boys, and Quebec is ours!"

The general led the way along a narrow path between the walls and the water, tripping and sliding on the blocks of ice thrown up onto land by the river's shifting tides. When the attackers reached a log wall blocking the route, soldiers ran forward with a saw and cut a hole. The men wriggled through. Then Montgomery took out his sword and waved it above his head—the signal to charge the next barricade, which guarded the road into the city.

They probably never saw the muzzle of the cannon sticking out from a hole in the barricade. The cannon exploded, shooting flames and a swarm of grapeshot—small iron balls designed to rip apart the sails of enemy ships. Montgomery was struck in both thighs, his cheek, his head, and was dead before he hit the snow. Eight other soldiers were killed by the blast. The survivors fell backward, away from city walls.

On the other side of the lower town, Arnold was out in front of his men, leading the way along the river to his own point of attack.

"It was impossible to bear up our faces against the imperious storm of wind and snow," said John Henry. The soldiers ran single file along the base of the wall, with the British firing straight down at them. The Americans could hardly see each other, let alone their enemy. "We could see nothing but the blaze from the muzzles of their muskets," said Henry.

As he felt his way forward, Henry's throat collided with a rope tied to a ship, sending him sprawling into a ditch. He climbed out and limped on. "Arnold called to the troops in a cheering voice," he said, "urging us forward."

Reaching the assigned place, Arnold motioned for the cannon, and men dragged it forward on a sled. Just as they were aiming the gun, there was a massive blast of musketry from inside the walls. Arnold felt something rip through the flesh below his knee.

"I received a wound by a ball through my left leg," he later reported, "which by loss of blood, rendered me very weak."

Arnold fell, got up, stumbled to the wall and leaned, unable to put any weight on the leg. Blood flowed into his boot and gurgled out into the snow. Soldiers raced over and held Arnold up.

"Hurry on!" he shouted to his army, "Hurry on, boys!"

Daniel Morgan ran forward, calling for men to carry Arnold back to the camp hospital. Arnold absolutely refused to be carried. Instead, he leaned heavily on two soldiers and hopped away from the walls. Some of the men stopped to look at their commander, but he shouted for them to get on with the fight.

The men ran forward with scaling ladders to continue the attack under Morgan.

"Daylight had scarce made its appearance 'ere Colonel Arnold was brought in," recalled Dr. Isaac Senter. Senter put Arnold on a table, tore away his pants, reached into his leg, and pulled out a flattened lead bullet. It must have ricocheted off a rock, Senter concluded, and from there into Arnold's leg below the knee and down into the heel, where it lodged. Senter showed the ball to Arnold, and told him amputation of the leg would probably be unnecessary.

Throughout the morning, wounded soldiers straggled back to the hospital, reporting that the British were pouring out from the city and headed for the American camp.

"Under these circumstances, we entreated Colonel Arnold for his own safety to be carried back into the country where they would not find him," Senter reported. "But to no purpose. He would neither be removed, nor suffer a man from the hospital to retreat. He ordered his pistols loaded, with a sword on his bed."

Arnold ordered all the other wounded men to be

given loaded guns. Then, propped up in bed, his leg wrapped in bloody bandages, pistols in his hands, he waited for the British attack, declaring he was "determined to kill as many as possible if they came into the room."

BLOCKADE IN THE SNOW
January 1–February 27, 1776

✤

The expected attack never came. Arnold lay in bed, listening to the sounds of fighting from Quebec. There was a lot of gunfire in the morning—something was happening—but then it slowed, and by afternoon there was quiet. The complete quiet of a world covered with snow.

Flat on his back, Arnold tried to write a letter. Of all people, he needed to contact David Wooster—the man he'd threatened in New Haven in order to get at the town's supply of gunpowder before marching his militia toward Boston. "For God's sake, order as many men down as you can possibly spare," Arnold implored Wooster, who was now in charge of American-held Montreal. "I hope you will stop every rascal who has deserted from us, and bring him back again."

Arnold apologized for the blunt nature of his note. "I am in such excessive pain from my wound," he wrote, "as the bones of my leg are affected."

It hurt even more when he thought of his failed battle plan. What had happened to Morgan's attack?

Finally, on the afternoon of the next day, Jonathan Meigs came into the hospital, guarded by a British soldier. Meigs was a prisoner of war now, he told Arnold. So was the entire force that had attacked under Arnold, those that were still alive. The British general, Guy Carleton, had allowed Meigs to come to camp to arrange the pick-up of the prisoners' baggage.

Meigs quickly told Arnold the story. After Arnold had limped away, the men raced up to the walls with ladders. Daniel Morgan was the first to jump onto a ladder and climb. Just as he got his head over the wall there was a tremendous blast and he fell backward into the snow. He just lay there for a while. Then he got up, blinking, his face stained with gunpowder, bleeding from the nose. He climbed back up the ladder and leaped over the wall screaming, "Quebec is ours!"

Three hundred Americans poured over the walls and into the city, soon reaching the spot where they were supposed to meet Montgomery's force. They knew

British soldiers would find them at any moment, and weren't sure what to do next. No one knew where any of the winding city streets led. "We took shelter from the fury of the storm under the sides of some of the buildings," Abner Stocking said.

A five-hundred-man British force was on its way, with Captain George Laws out in front—farther out front than he realized. He charged up to the Americans and shouted, "You are all my prisoners!"

Morgan's men were confused. "How your prisoners?" they asked. "You are ours."

"No, no, my dear creatures," said Laws, "I vow of God you are all mine, don't mistake yourselves."

"But where are your men?"

"O, ho, make yourselves easy about that matter, they are all about here, and will be with you in a twinkling."

And they were. Suddenly finding themselves surrounded by gunfire, Morgan's men spread out, taking cover in doorways and alleys. "Our men were mowed down in heaps," Stocking said.

John Lamb was shot in the cheek. He pulled out a handkerchief, tied up the hole in his face, and went on fighting. Archibald Steele had two fingers blown off his hand. Men kicked in doors and dove into houses, and still weren't safe. John Henry saw a friend take a bullet in the chest. "He staggered a few feet backwards and fell upon a bed, where he instantly expired."

The Americans tried to shoot back, but couldn't. "Neither I, nor one in ten of my men could get off our guns they being so exceeding wet," said Henry Dearborn.

In the midst of this chaos a British soldier spotted Dearborn and shouted, "Who are you?"

"A friend," Dearborn said.

"Friend to who?"

"To liberty."

To which the British soldier replied, "Goddamn you!" and raised his gun. Dearborn had no choice but to surrender.

By ten that morning the entire force had been shot or captured. All except Daniel Morgan. Standing with a stone wall at his back—the back that had taken 499 lashes from a British whip—Morgan swung his sword wildly, tears of rage running down his face, as he shouted his refusal to surrender. No one wanted to get any closer to him. Then Morgan spotted, among the mass of soldiers around him, a man in a priest's outfit.

"Are you a priest?" Morgan called out.

Yes, the man said.

"Then I give my sword to you," said Morgan. "But

not a scoundrel of these cowards shall take it out of my hands."

In the weeks following the attack, Arnold hopped around on crutches, directing a siege of Quebec with what was left of his and Montgomery's armies. "I have no thoughts of leaving this proud town until I first enter it in triumph," Arnold wrote to his sister back in New Haven.

David Wooster, from the comfort of his headquarters in Montreal, was impressed, reporting to Washington, "Arnold has, to his great honor, kept up the blockade with such a handful of men, that the story, when told hereafter, will be scarcely credited."

It was not much of a blockade, though. Many of the soldiers had headed home when their enlistments ended in January. Arnold didn't have nearly enough men to actually keep supplies from reaching the city. In fact, his force was so badly outnumbered that the British could have come out and destroyed him at any time. Luckily it was too cold. Temperatures plunged to thirty degrees below zero—too cold to fight, too cold even to stand guard. A British officer realized this one morning when he walked up to a soldier who had been standing at his post all night.

"God bless your honor," said the guard. "I am glad you are come for I am blind."

"On the officer's examining him," another soldier said, "he found the man's eyes had watered with the severity of the cold and that his eyelids were froze together." The guard was carried inside and set down near a fire.

While Arnold held on in Canada, news of his march to Quebec, and the desperate battle for the city, started reaching people in the American Colonies. General Schuyler captured the reaction of amazed Americans everywhere, saying, "Colonel Arnold's march does him great honor; some future historian will make it the subject of admiration to his readers."

"The merit of this gentleman is certainly great," Washington agreed. "I heartily wish that fortune may distinguish him as one of her favorites."

Washington wrote to Arnold, letting him know he'd been promoted to general. "My thanks are due, and sincerely offered to you, for your enterprising and persevering spirit," said Washington.

"I am greatly obliged to you for your good wishes, and the concern you express for me," Arnold wrote back. "I have the pleasure to inform you my wound is entirely healed, and I am able to hobble about my room, though my leg is a little contracted and weak. I hope soon to be fit for action." In the meantime, he assured Washington, he would stay and continue the siege.

But it could end only one way, Arnold knew. His small army was suffering from frostbite, flu, pneumonia, and, as the winter wore on, smallpox. Arnold was nearly out of supplies and completely out of money. And as soon as the St. Lawrence thawed, thousands of British soldiers were sure to arrive by ship. That would be the end of Arnold's dream of taking Canada.

By late February, Arnold was worn out, mentally and physically. This comes through in a letter he sent to Washington, a rare private moment in which he exposed his inner doubts. "The severity of the climate, the troops very illy clad, and worse paid," he began. "In short, the choice of difficulties I have had to encounter, has rendered it so very perplexing, that I have often been at a loss how to conduct matters."

Arnold was ready to turn over his army to a more senior general. "The service," he said, "requires a person of greater abilities and experience than I can pretend to."

ANDRÉ IN PENNSYLVANIA
January–July 1776

❧

John André, prisoner of war, traveled south through a blizzard. Late one night he reached an inn by the shores of Lake George, just a small log cabin with a sign outside. He went in. He heard the sounds of snoring men, smelled the bodies, and when his eyes adjusted to the dark he saw that the floor was covered with mattresses, and the mattresses crowded with sleepers.

The innkeeper tiptoed over and pointed out a mattress with only one body. Tripping over hands and faces to get there, André stripped off his soaking uniform and slipped under the covers beside an enormous man. At least it was warm.

The man rolled over and greeted André. They started whispering back and forth, and the conversation quickly turned interesting. André was pleasantly surprised—his bedfellow knew books, poetry, music, and history. They talked all night.

At dawn, everyone stood up and started dressing. André put on his British uniform, and the big man put on an American uniform. The American introduced himself as Henry Knox, former bookseller, current Continental Army officer on a mission for George Washington. He was on his way to Fort Ticonderoga to get a bunch of cannon that had been captured by Benedict Arnold and Ethan Allen last spring.

The new friends wished each other luck, and then headed off in different directions.

André sailed down the icy Hudson River to New York City, and then went by land to report to Congress in Philadelphia.

After months in the backwoods, he was thrilled to find himself in a real town. Philadelphia was the biggest city in America, with busy streets, theaters, shops, good food, and, most important, elegantly dressed, beautiful women. He met many of the charming ladies, including a sixteen-year-old blonde named Peggy Shippen. He and Peggy spoke only briefly—but they would remember each other.

Sadly, André had no time to linger; he was a prisoner

of war. He was ordered to get back on the road and head to Lancaster, about eighty miles to the west, where he would be held until further notice.

André reached Lancaster in late February 1776. Angry townspeople watched him walk through town. Many other British prisoners were already there—common soldiers were held in barracks, but officers were expected to find their own quarters. This was a problem, since no local families would have them.

André took a room at a tavern, and tried to adjust to life in what seemed to him the middle of nowhere. He played his flute and read poetry. To kill time he offered drawing classes to local children. "I often played marbles and other boyish games with the major," remembered one child.

But in March, just as André was settling in, a new order came. British officers were to be scattered to smaller towns, to prevent them from plotting together. André was told to move on to Carlisle, Pennsylvania. He climbed onto a wagon and bounced down a dirt path, forty miles deeper into the forest.

Carlisle made Lancaster look like London. André saw maybe two hundred wooden cabins on cleared dirt patches in the thick, dark woods. Even worse, this town had sent many young men to the war—several of them survived Arnold's march to Quebec, only to die storming the city. A man in a British uniform was not welcome here.

André moved into a tavern, sharing his room with Captain John Despard, a fellow prisoner who happened to play a little violin. "Myself and Mr. Despard are much engaged in playing duets," André wrote.

There wasn't much else to do. "We seldom have conversation with them," André said of the people of Carlisle, "because generally no good result§ from it— nothing but uncivil and hostile answers."

One local resident remembered André as "a very handsome young man," who rarely left his room. "He used to sit and read with his feet on the wainscot of the window, where two beautiful pointer dogs laid their heads on his feet."

One day, sick of being inside, André and Despard decided to do a little hunting. Imprisoned officers were never actually locked up, and were allowed to go six miles into the woods, provided they gave their word, as gentlemen, they would not escape.

Still, people in town kept suspicious eyes on the British officers as they headed through town holding muskets. A woman known to history only as "Mrs. Ramsay" spotted

André handing a letter to a local resident, one suspected of having Loyalist leanings. She spread the alarm, and several men ran out, seized the letter, tore it open, and gathered round to read it.

"It's in code!" they shouted.

André rolled his eyes. The letter was written in French, he explained.

It was an innocent letter he was hoping to have delivered to a friend, but none of the men read French. They ordered André and Despard to hand over their hunting guns, and stay in town from then on. The officers smashed their muskets to the ground.

"No damn Rebel should ever burn powder in them!" grumbled Despard.

That night a group of armed militiamen, roaring drunk, gathered by the window of André and Despard's room. Swaying and cursing, they called for the Redcoats to draw swords and die like men.

André and Despard were preparing to do just that, when Mrs. Ramsay came running out of her house in her nightshirt and nightcap, waving a broom. She knew the militia leader, who'd once been an apprentice to her husband. She told him to go home and sober up.

"You may thank my old mistress for your lives!" the

THE NOTORIOUS BENEDICT ARNOLD

man shouted, as he and the others tripped back into the darkness.

The next day André sent Mrs. Ramsay a box of expensive candles. She sent them back with a short note, saying she could accept nothing from a British officer.

"We were every day pelted and reviled in the streets," André wrote to his mother, "and have been oftentimes invited to smell a brandished hatchet and reminded of its agreeable effects on the skull, receiving at the same time promises that we should be murdered before the next day."

Unable to fight back, André contented himself with inventing witty insults, calling the locals "perfidious dastards," in one letter, and, in other, "a greasy committee of worsted-stocking knaves." He could do nothing else. Nothing but lay low, and wait—and dream of revenge.

THE LAST MAN OUT
May 6–July 28, 1776

❧

Congress sent a new general, John Thomas, to take command at Quebec. When Thomas arrived, Arnold traveled to Montreal to rest and recover.

Thomas hoped to make a stand outside Quebec, but he had a camp full of exhausted, sick soldiers. Then he caught smallpox himself. And then, just as the ice on the St. Lawrence River began to break up, came the British.

On the morning of May 6, an American guard spotted the British warship *Surprise* coming toward Quebec, crashing through chunks of floating ice. It was just the first of fifteen ships, carrying more than ten thousand Redcoats.

This sparked a nightmarish retreat. American soldiers raced along the riverbank toward Montreal, chased by British warships lobbing bombs and spraying grapeshot into the chaotic crowds. General Thomas left so quickly that when the British general Guy Carleton came charging out of the city, he found supper still warm on Thomas's table.

At Montreal, Benedict Arnold watched the panicked troops turning south to follow the route back toward New York. He could see that the men didn't have enough supplies for the long retreat ahead. Arnold seized food, blankets, and clothing from merchants in Montreal, leaving behind IOUs promising that Congress would eventually pay for everything. Then he followed the retreating army.

Arnold sent the supplies south to St. John's with orders for Colonel Moses Hazen to take charge of them. But Hazen disliked Arnold, considered Arnold bossy and reckless, and refused to take responsibility for the provisions. Instead, he left them unguarded beside the road. Retreating soldiers simply grabbed what they needed as they hurried past.

Arnold had carefully labeled each package with the name of the store it had come from, so that each merchant could be reimbursed. Now there was no way of knowing who was owed what, making the Americans look like thieves. When he saw the empty crates, Arnold cursed Moses Hazen to his face. "This is not the first or last order Colonel Hazen has disobeyed," he grumbled.

Badly offended, Hazen leaped at the opportunity to smear his enemy, spreading the story that Arnold had looted Montreal for his own private gain.

By June 18 the entire army had passed St. John's and was rowing south toward Lake Champlain. The entire army except Benedict Arnold, and his young aide, James Wilkinson. "I am content to be the last man who quits this country," Arnold declared. A nervous Wilkinson was somewhat less content.

As the British army approached, Arnold stayed behind to make sure every building was set on fire. Late that afternoon, with black smoke rising from the ruins of St. John's, Arnold heard the crash of army drums, the shouts of officers urging men forward, the thunder of thousands of feet pounding the dirt road.

Wilkinson was starting to panic. He and Arnold galloped their horses to the edge of the river, where one last canoe was tied up. Just as the first British soldiers broke out of the woods, Arnold jumped down from his horse. Determined to leave nothing of use behind, he quickly stripped the saddle off the horse, tossed it in the boat, pulled out his pistol, held it to the horse's head, and pulled the trigger. Wilkinson shuddered. But Arnold, he said, "ordered me to follow his example, which I did with reluctance."

Then, as British bullets smacked the ground and water around them, Arnold gestured toward the canoe, and Wilkinson jumped in. Arnold pushed the boat into the river, leaped in, and grabbed a paddle. As promised, he was the last man out of Canada.

That night he caught up with the retreating army on an island in the river. Candles lit a scene of horror— soldiers dragging bodies to large open pits, while other men, clinging to life, lay helpless on the ground.

"Language cannot describe nor imagination paint, the scenes of misery and distress the soldiery endure," said Dr. Lewis Beebe, who was fighting what had become an epidemic of smallpox. "The most shocking of all spectacles," he said, "was to see a large barn crowded full of men with this disorder, many of which could not see, speak, or walk—one, nay two had large maggots, an inch long, crawl out of their ears."

In the morning the sick men were loaded onto boats, and the army moved south. This continued all the way to the forts at Crown Point and Ticonderoga. Here, finally, the Americans could take a breath.

Not a long one. Everyone knew a massive British attack was close behind.

On a hot and buggy day in early July, five top Northern Army generals gathered at Crown Point, and were shocked at what they saw. Dying men lay everywhere, and healthy soldiers were in no mood to take orders. As Dr. Beebe reported: "The soldiers [are] either sleeping, swimming, fishing, or cursing and swearing—most generally the latter."

The generals walked into a meeting room, led by Philip Schuyler, commander of the Northern Army. Right behind him was Horatio Gates, who felt *he* should be the man in charge. Schuyler and Gates despised each other, and their rivalry would turn increasingly nasty in the coming year, but for now Schuyler was on top. It was with tremendous pleasure that he lowered himself into the only comfortable armchair in the room. Gates and the others sat on benches around the table.

Pointing to maps as he talked, Benedict Arnold reviewed the situation. Spies had reported that thousands of British soldiers and sailors, along with Indian allies, were gathering at St. John's. The British were building a fleet of at least twenty-five warships—some of them were actually built in Britain, taken apart and labeled, hauled overland to St. John's, and put back together for use on Lake Champlain. When the fleet was ready, the next steps were obvious. They would blow the Americans off the lake, move to the Hudson River, and blast their way to the Atlantic Ocean at New York City. The Colonies would be sliced in two, and probably wouldn't survive for long after that.

The British fleet must be stopped right there on Lake Champlain, Arnold argued. The British needed time to finish their ships, he pointed out, possibly as much as two months. That might give the Americans time to build a fleet of their own.

Arnold took out some drawings he'd been working on and passed them around. The sketches showed row galleys, he explained, about seventy feet long, with cannon around the sides. The boats would have two sails, but they could also be rowed, making them quicker and easier to turn than the bigger British ships, and better in shallow lake water. The Americans would be badly outgunned, and the British navy was the best in the world, which meant their crews would be battle-tested veterans. But the Americans could worry about that later—first they had to build the boats.

Schuyler, Gates, and the other generals were silent. They were not sure what they could possibly add.

⌒

"General Arnold, who is perfectly skilled in naval affairs, has most nobly undertaken to command our fleet upon the lake," Gates reported to Congress.

"I am extremely happy that General Arnold has undertaken to command the fleet," Schuyler added. "It has relieved me from very great anxiety."

For once in their lives Gates and Schuyler agreed on something—this was a job for Benedict Arnold. They were glad to let Arnold take the responsibility for the coming battle—and, very possibly, the blame.

Newly appointed Commander of the Lakes, Arnold got busy building America's first naval fleet. As work got under way, a messenger arrived from Philadelphia with something called the Declaration of Independence. Soldiers stopped hammering and sawing long enough to listen to it read aloud.

" 'We hold these truths to be self-evident,' " an officer read from the document, " 'that all men are created equal, that they are endowed by their Creator with certain unalienable rights, that among these are life, liberty and the pursuit of happiness . . .' "

The workers stood, sweating and swatting mosquitoes, as the reader droned on, reciting an endless list of complaints against King George III. Then, finally, he got to the point. "'We, therefore, the representatives of the United States of America, in general Congress assembled, appealing to the Supreme Judge of the world for the rectitude of our intentions, do, in the name, and by authority of the good people of these Colonies, solemnly publish and declare, that these united Colonies are, and of right ought to be free and independent states.'"

Arnold's men gave a cheer. The United States of America—that sounded pretty good. Now all they had to do was make it a reality.

ARNOLD'S MOTLEY CREW
August 1–October 11, 1776

❧

Over the next few weeks, Arnold followed the news from Washington's main army. It was not encouraging. Camped at New York City, Washington's untrained troops were about to face an overwhelming British attack. "We expect a bloody summer in New York," he said, "and I am sorry to say that we are not, either in men or arms, prepared for it."

This only increased the pressure on Arnold. He spent his days sailing around the lake, checking on his men—he had teams chopping down trees, teams sawing planks, teams hammering ships together at waterside boatyards. He divided crews into day and night shifts and kept things moving twenty-four hours a day. But it was all going too slowly. He needed more ship carpenters, more ammunition, more nails. Most of all, he needed some experienced sailors.

Arnold fired off endless requests to Gates. "If you want breeches, they give you a vest," complained Arnold. "As for sailors, they give you tavern waiters."

"Believe me, dear sir," Gates assured Arnold, "no man alive could be more anxious for the welfare of you and your fleet."

Gates then forwarded Arnold's demands on to Schuyler, saying: "Pray hurry it up. The moments are precious, and not one of them should be lost."

Arnold, frustrated and tactless, went over Gates's head and sent requests for supplies straight to Schuyler. As the days flew past and the tension mounted, the three generals grew increasingly annoyed with each other.

Meanwhile, Moses Hazen was still spreading the rumor that Arnold had robbed the shopkeepers of Montreal. It was a serious charge, and the army formed a special court at Ticonderoga to investigate. Gates told Arnold he'd better go testify. "I cannot but think it extremely cruel," Arnold groaned, "when I have sacrificed my ease, health, and great part of my private property in the cause of country, to be calumniated as a robber and thief."

With the time bomb of the coming battle ticking in his head, Arnold was forced to spend a tortuous week in court. "The whole of the general's conduct during the course of the trial was marked with contempt and disrespect toward the court," the judges reported. Describing Arnold's behavior as "ungentleman-like," they demanded an apology.

Arnold's response was not quite what they had in mind. "As your very nice and delicate honor, in your apprehension, is injured," he told the court, "you may depend, as soon as this disagreeable hearing is at an end, which God grant may soon be the case, I will by no means withhold from any gentleman of the court the satisfaction his nice honor may require."

Arnold was challenging the judges to duel—all of them. The officers, offended and frightened, requested that Gates have Arnold placed under arrest.

In a beautiful understatement, Gates acknowledged, "the warmth of General Arnold's temper might possibly lead him a little further than is marked by the precise line of decorum." But with the British fleet massing on Lake Champlain, Gates could not spare Arnold. "I was obliged to act dictatorially, and dissolve the court-martial," he said. "The United States must not be deprived of that excellent officer's service at this important moment."

And so the whole thing was brushed under the carpet—but forgotten by no one.

There was yet another distraction that summer, this one in the form of a rotund officer named Jacobus Wyncoop. Schuyler had put Wyncoop in charge of Lake Champlain earlier in the year, when there was nothing to do. Now, with the war coming, Wyncoop refused to accept that he was no longer in command.

He tooled around the lake, overruling Arnold's orders. At one point that summer he suddenly declared he would sail north and take on the British. He cruised partway to Canada, spotted the sail of a British warship, turned around, and raced home. It turned out the British sail was actually a flock of seagulls.

One day in August, Arnold sent a few boats to pick up a crew of men who had been chopping wood by the lake. Wyncoop sailed up to Arnold's boats, ordered them to stop, and even fired a warning shot across their bows. Declaring himself to be Commodore of the Lake, he passed on a message for Arnold: "I know no orders but what shall be given out by me."

Arnold watched the whole thing from shore through his spyglass. He jumped onto his own boat, raced to Wyncoop, and demanded an explanation, saying, "I am surprised you should pretend to contradict my orders."

"I am resolved to go under the orders of no man," Wyncoop replied.

Luckily for Wyncoop, Arnold seemed more stunned than angry. "You surely must be out of your senses to say no orders shall be obeyed but yours," said Arnold. Wyncoop had better stop interfering, Arnold said, or "I shall be under the disagreeable necessity of convincing you of your error by immediately arresting you."

Arnold was, soon after, under that "necessity." Wyncoop was sent to Gates, who booted him out of the army. Wyncoop later showed up in Philadelphia, where he began spreading nasty stories about Arnold.

In September, Arnold's spies came back to camp with the news that the British were planning to launch their attack within a month.

"I beg at least one hundred good seamen as soon as possible," Arnold wrote to Gates. "We have a wretched motley crew in the fleet." Reluctant soldiers had drawn lots to see who would have to serve with Arnold—thus the "motley crew." Arnold also begged for more ammunition, gunpowder, guns, grenades, ropes, and rum.

"Be satisfied," pleaded Gates. "More cannot be done than is done."

On October 1 Arnold wrote what he called a "memorandum of articles, which have been repeatedly written for, and which we are in the most extreme want of." He was beginning to realize that no one thought the Americans could win the coming battle—and that maybe he was being set up to take the fall. "I hope to be excused," he wrote, "if with five hundred men, half naked, I should not be able to beat the enemy with seven thousand men."

He wrote his will, and sent it to his sister.

Working with what he had, Arnold trained his men, trying to teach them the discipline needed to run a ship. When he caught sailors napping at their posts, each was given, according to one of the crew, "twelve strokes on his naked buttocks."

Arnold had just enough ammunition to let his men fire a few practice rounds from the ships. After firing one of the cannons, a sailor named Solomon Dyer sponged out the muzzle to extinguish any sparks. He must have missed one. As he rammed a new gunpowder cartridge into the muzzle, the other men heard an explosion, and saw Dyer blown overboard. His body bobbed in the water, the sponging rod blown clear through his chest. A few feet away floated his hands.

The gruesome message was clear: Arnold could not fight a textbook naval battle with this crew; he couldn't take on British ships in the open water. He'd have to come up with something more creative.

Snow soon covered the mountains around the lake. Arnold moved his little fleet behind Valcour Island, near the New York shore. "Every ship keeps half their men constantly on deck, under arms and matches lighted," he reported. "It will be impossible for the enemy to surprise us."

Arnold paced in his cabin, waiting for battle. On his desk was a letter with news from General Washington, and it was bad—the army had been beaten at New York City and was now retreating, running for its life. There was also a letter from Hannah, telling him that she'd received his will. She added a message from Arnold's youngest son. "Little Hal sends a kiss to Pa and says, 'Auntie, tell my papa he must come home, I want to kiss him.'"

The morning of October 11 was cold and clear. As the British fleet sailed south on the lake, General Guy

Carleton and a naval captain named Thomas Pringle stood on the deck of their ship. There were no American ships in sight, and Pringle was disappointed.

"The rascals won't give us a chance to burn powder," Pringle grunted.

Carleton had seen Benedict Arnold in action at Quebec. Without taking his eyes from the lake, he said, "Wait and see."

BATTLE OF VALCOUR ISLAND
October 11, 1776

❦

Arnold's fleet of fifteen small ships was arranged in an arc, hiding in a narrow channel between Valcour Island and the main shore of Lake Champlain. A sharp wind blew from the north. Flapping from the masts were newly designed flags—a coiled rattlesnake on a bright yellow background, and in black print the warning, "Don't Tread on Me."

Just after eight in the morning, a young sailor named Bayze Wells spotted an American boat, the men aboard paddling furiously toward the fleet. "The guard boat came in and fired an alarm and brought news," Wells said.

Arnold rushed on deck to hear the report: the British fleet was in sight. "We immediately prepared to receive them," he said.

✍

As planned, the captains of the American fleet raced to Arnold's ship, *Congress*, for a quick strategy session. They crowded into a tiny cabin crammed with barrels and cannonballs.

Arnold reviewed the situation. The Americans had fifteen ships manned by about eight hundred men. The British had a total of thirty-four ships of different sizes, with about seven hundred experienced sailors, plus hundreds more soldiers and Indian warriors. The British fleet had more guns and could fire a lot more metal— just one of the British warships had six guns that fired twenty-four-pound balls. Arnold's whole fleet didn't have a single gun that big.

Knowing he didn't have the firepower or the crew to fight the British on the open lake, Arnold had tucked the fleet behind Valcour Island. The island was hilly and wooded, about two miles long, one wide, and half a mile from the shore. Ships coming from the north would not be able to see into the channel behind the island; this was the key to Arnold's plan. The British, he hoped, would sail right past. Then, when they finally spotted the Americans, they'd have to turn around, they'd have to beat against the wind to get into the channel where Arnold's ships were anchored. That would give the

Americans their chance—their small, quick boats could dash out and blast away at the bigger, clumsier British warships.

There was one problem with the plan, and everyone in Arnold's cabin saw it: the entire American fleet was sitting in a death trap. If the wind changed direction, the British ships could race into the channel and easily destroy the Americans. There was no escape route—the other end of the channel was too shallow for ships to pass.

"I gave it as my opinion," said David Waterbury, "that the fleet ought immediately to come to sail and fight them on the retreat in the main lake."

Arnold shook his head. The American crews couldn't handle a running naval battle, and the British ships would be faster on the open lake.

As the men left the cabin, Arnold reminded them to drape wet blankets over their powder barrels to protect from flying sparks. He also told them to have their men spread sand over the decks of their ships.

One of the officers asked why.

So the men won't slip on the blood, Arnold explained.

Standing on the deck of the *Congress* at 10:00 a.m., Arnold saw that he had won his first roll of the dice. As

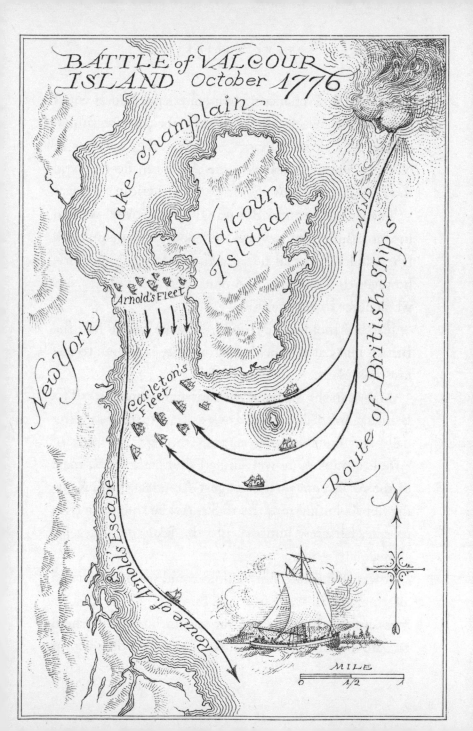

expected, the British were overconfident. Sailing without scouting vessels, they cruised right past the southern end of Valcour Island. Only when they were south of the island did they spot the American fleet behind them.

The British commander was annoyed. "After we had in this manner got beyond the enemy," Carleton said, "the wind which had been favorable to bring us there, however entirely prevented our being able to bring our whole force to engage them."

Just as Arnold had planned. Now he had to lure the British into battle quickly, before they had time to adjust their plans.

American ships darted forward and opened fire. The British ships began firing back as they turned, sending balls and metal chains ripping through the sails of Arnold's ships. One well-aimed shot cracked the mast of the *Royal Savage*, the biggest American ship, sending her slamming into the rocks. As the ship turned on its side, her crew jumped into the lake and swam for shore.

It was a bad start, but Arnold could see that the men all around him were fighting furiously. "The engagement became general, and very warm," he said. Arnold ran around the deck of his ship, barking orders over crashing explosions, aiming and firing the guns himself as fast as they could be loaded.

"Close to one o'clock in the afternoon, this naval battle began to get very serious," said a German officer serving with the British. Some British ships were still struggling to get into position, but most of the boats on both sides were in the action, blasting at each other in the crowded bay. "Very fierce," said a British captain, "very animated."

British sailors stoked furnaces on deck, heating their cannonballs to glowing red before firing them. Boarding parties jumped into bateaux and paddled toward the Americans. Arnold's men blasted the boats to pieces, filling the choppy water with burning wood and men struggling to stay afloat.

One of Arnold's shots sent an eighteen-pound ball screaming toward General Carleton on his ship, *Maria*. The ball just missed Carleton, smashed into the deck, and knocked out Carleton's brother Thomas, who lay flat on his back, bleeding from his ears.

Trying to play it cool, Carleton turned to a surgeon and said, "Well, Doctor, how do you like a sea fight?"

But everyone could see he was shaken. This was not the battle he had pictured.

❧

The fighting raged all afternoon. "The enemy fleet attacked ours with great fury," said Pascal De Angelis, a thirteen-year-old American volunteer. "And we returned the fire with as great a spirit and vigor and the most desperate cannonading."

The air was filled with smoke, the smell of gunpowder, and the echoing boom of big guns. Cannonballs crashed into ships on both sides, sending limbs flying, leaving dead and unconscious men lying in spreading puddles of blood.

One shot hit the powder magazine on a British ship, sparking a massive explosion that killed half the crew. The Americans cheered, then reloaded.

On the American ship *New York* the men held a match to a cannon touchhole, but instead of firing, the gun burst and hot metal splinters sliced through the crew.

All over the American fleet, bodies were tossed overboard to get them out of the way—and to keep them from spreading panic among those still fighting.

Arnold's crews were getting shot at from land as well. "The enemy landed a large number of Indians on the island and each shore, who kept up an incessant fire on us," Arnold said. A few of his best marksmen tied themselves to the tops of masts and fired back. When one of these men was hit, he swung back and forth, his leg still tied to the mast, dripping blood on the men below.

As the sun set that night, the superior British firepower was beginning to win out. When the firing died down, Carleton sent men to set the abandoned *Royal Savage* on fire. Huge orange flames lit up the dark bay, and from the deck of his ship Arnold could see that the British were settling in for the night, blocking the Americans in the channel.

The American captains gathered again on the *Congress*. Arnold's ship had twenty holes blown in its sides, but it was no worse off than most of the others. His cabin had been used for an operating room, and there was dried blood everywhere.

Surrounded by the thick smell of blood, the captains took turns reviewing their casualty figures and the condition of their ships. The officers' ears were aching and pounding from the day's explosions, and they had to practically scream to be heard. The news was grim. Every ship was badly damaged—one of them, the *Philadelphia*, actually sank as they were meeting. At least sixty men had been killed, and many more wounded. The fleet's ammunition was three-fourths gone. In the morning, the British could easily wipe them out.

Arnold calmly reviewed their three options. First was to stay and fight—madness, given their condition. Second was to surrender—not worth consideration. Third, well . . . the British had left a small gap between their line of ships and the New York shore. Arnold had spent months studying and mapping the lake. He knew the water in that gap was just deep enough for his ships.

The third option was to try a midnight escape.

THE REVOLUTION LIVES
October 12–November 2, 1776

🐚

The American captains returned to their ships and ordered their men to carry the wounded below deck. With any luck, the British wouldn't hear them moaning as the Americans slipped past.

The night was dark and moonless. Each captain lit a low flame in a lantern and covered the sides of the lantern with cloth, making the faint light visible only from directly behind. One lantern was hung at the back of each boat. The men wrapped shirts around the ships' oars to muffle their sound, and, very gently, dipped the oars into the lake.

Colonel Edward Wigglesworth led the way, and the other captains followed in single file, each guided by the dim light on the boat ahead. Amazed and breathless as he glided past the British ships, Wigglesworth could easily hear sailors talking, carpenters hammering. "We rowed out clear of the enemy without being discovered," he said.

Arnold, on the *Congress*, was the last to leave.

When the sun rose the next morning the British discovered that their trap was empty.

"General Carleton was in a rage," one sailor remembered. Cursing and shouting to cover his embarrassment, Carleton ordered his ships to turn around and chase down Arnold's fleet.

By that point Arnold had an eight-mile head start. "On the whole, I think we have had a very fortunate escape," he reported.

Now it was a race to Crown Point, thirty-five miles to the south. If Arnold could get there, the fort's guns and soldiers would protect him. On the open lake, he was dead.

Some men rowed, some frantically repaired masts and sails, and some bailed just to keep the leaky ships from going down. The wind blew hard all day, bringing sleet and rain. Arnold's fleet stayed ahead of the British, rowing through a second straight sleepless night.

By morning they could see the bigger British warships

closing in. "The enemy came hard against us," said Bayze Wells. They were still twenty miles from Crown Point.

The British caught Arnold's fleet at noon. For the next two hours the Americans continued rowing south as fast as they could, with the British following close behind, blowing hole after hole in the retreating ships.

"The sails, rigging, and hull of the *Congress* were shattered and torn in pieces," Arnold said. None of his ships could stay afloat much longer. Arnold's expert knowledge of the lake paid off again—he knew they were approaching a shallow, rocky bay, where the British ships couldn't follow. At Arnold's signal, his men ran their ships into the rocks and leaped out into the water. They carried the wounded to shore, then went back and lit their ships on fire. Flames spread up the masts and jumped onto the sails. Above the flames, still whipping in the wind, were the fleet's yellow rattlesnake flags.

The fire on the *Congress* reached a powder keg, which exploded, killing a badly wounded officer who'd been left behind in the chaos. The men watched his broken body tumble high into the air and crash down in the lake. Arnold cursed furiously, then urged his men up the banks and into the woods. They were still more than ten miles from Crown Point.

Marching all day, carrying the wounded on stretchers and on their backs, the army reached Crown Point that night. But the main army had already abandoned the place and fallen back to Fort Ticonderoga, which was in better condition. Arnold and the men continued on to Fort Ti, finally collapsing at the fort at four in the morning.

"I reached this place extremely fatigued and unwell," Arnold said, "having been without sleep or refreshment for near three days."

"The whole body of the enemy are now within two hours march of us," said General Anthony Wayne at Fort Ticonderoga. "We expect to see them every moment."

There were thousands of well-rested soldiers at Fort Ti. Rested, but scared—they knew they didn't have enough ammunition to fight off the coming attack.

Then, surprisingly, a day passed, and nothing happened. Then another day. "I expect this stillness will be succeeded immediately by a grand attack," said Gates.

It wasn't. On October 25, ten days after Arnold's arrival, all was still eerily quiet. "Mr. Carleton has not yet made us a visit," said one officer, "which surprises me very much."

Three days later American scouts finally spotted Carleton's ships on the lake. They took a few shots at the British, but the ships were too far away to hit.

Carleton stood on the deck of his ship, studying the American fort through his spyglass, feeling cautious. He had no idea how strong the fort was. It was late in the year to be starting a new attack, and his supply lines to Canada were dangerously long. Besides, his own fleet had taken a pounding in the unexpectedly violent tangle with Arnold. It was enough for one season, Carleton decided.

"The rebel fleet upon Lake Champlain has been entirely defeated in two actions," he reported to London. That was true, but Carleton was supposed to have blown the Americans off the lake and then driven inland. The following year, British forces would have to begin their invasion all over again.

On November 2, with snow flurries swirling, Carleton turned his ships back toward Canada. From Fort Ticonderoga, Gates watched the fleet disappear. "Lake

Champlain is closed with ice," he reported to Congress just a few weeks later. "All is secure in that quarter until the beginning of May."

Benedict Arnold's little navy was gone. But it had kept the American Revolution alive.

ANDRÉ FIGHTS ON
November 1776–April 1777

John André was resigned to spending the coming winter in the wilds of Pennsylvania. He'd been hearing rumors of a prisoner exchange, but they were just rumors.

Then, on the morning of November 28, he was ordered to gather his things and prepare for a march. Unsure of where he was headed, he chose to be hopeful. "We are on our road," he wrote, "as we believe, to be exchanged."

Guarded by Americans, André and several other British prisoners set out on foot. André quickly realized they were moving east—the way to civilization. Over the next few days he filled pages of his notebook with notes on local geography. A young girl at an inn where the prisoners stayed remembered that he "spent most of his time in examining and drawing charts and maps of the country."

Trudging through deep snow, the prisoners crossed New Jersey and were set loose near British lines. On December 10, André arrived in New York City, which the British had taken from Washington a few months before.

"I am in perfect health, am in a good house by a good fire," he wrote to his mother. After more than a year as a prisoner of war, and several close calls, he could hardly believe he was free again. "You may conclude my carcass to be very safe for this winter, and, as I have some regard for myself, you may depend upon it I shall do my utmost to make myself as happy and comfortable as I can."

This was a key turning point in André's life. Other officers in his regiment began heading back home, and André was eligible to return as well. A year ago he'd have leaped at the chance to continue his army service back in Britain. Now things had changed. Now he had a score to settle with the Americans.

When General William Howe arrived to take command of British forces in America, André sent Howe the notes and maps he'd made in Pennsylvania. Howe was impressed with the quality of André's work—it would come in very handy if the British were to invade that area. Howe promised to help André find a good position in his army.

André spent a relaxing winter in Staten Island. In spring he was assigned to the staff of General Charles Grey, an officer known for his aggressive attacking style. Convinced the British had been taking it too easy on the Americans, Grey was determined to show these rebels what war was really like.

It was exactly what André was looking for. "I am in the most happy situation with my general," he said.

A QUESTION OF HONOR
January 4–April 25, 1777

✦

Benedict Arnold's sister, Hannah, and his three sons were part of the huge crowd that lined the streets of New Haven, cheering and waving flags, as Arnold rode back into town.

Arnold hopped down from his carriage and took in the scene. Veterans of the march to Quebec—recently released in the prisoner exchange that had freed André—stepped out to greet him. The men stood in the street, hugging and crying.

Back at home, Arnold was able to catch up on some reading on his favorite subject. "General Arnold and his troops conducted themselves during their action with great firmness and intrepidity," reported the *Philadelphia Gazette*, "and made a better resistance than could have been expected against a force so greatly superior."

"Few men ever met with so many hairbreadth escapes in so short a space of time," General Gates said of Arnold, going on to praise him and his men "for the gallant defense they made against the great superiority of the enemy's force. Such magnanimous behavior will establish the fame of American arms throughout the globe."

Even the British were impressed. "I am sorry you did not get Arnold," the British secretary of state wrote to Carleton. "I think he has shown himself the most enterprising and dangerous man among the rebels."

Arnold noticed that even his neighbors' attitudes had changed. People who recently considered themselves too good to associate with him were now coming over uninvited, just to ask how he was, congratulate him, and wish him well.

The same thing happened when he visited Boston that winter—the fanciest people in town smiled at Arnold, shook his hand, clapped his back. He was invited to all the best parties, including one at the home of Henry Knox—the American officer who'd once shared a mattress with John André.

It was here that Arnold met sixteen-year-old Elizabeth DeBlois, "the belle of Boston," as she was then known.

"She puckers her mouth a little," said one local man, "and contracts her eyelids a little to look very pretty, and is not wholly unsuccessful." Benedict and Elizabeth flirted all night—with her mother looking on and, to judge by appearances, not at all approving.

Hardly discouraged by the mother, Arnold bought an expensive trunk of gowns for "My dear Betsy," as he called her. He had them delivered to Henry Knox's wife, Lucy, along with a note. "I have taken the liberty of enclosing a letter to the heavenly Miss DeBlois," he wrote to Lucy Knox, "which I beg the favor of your delivering with the trunk of gowns." At the end of the note he added: "I shall remain under the most anxious suspense."

As he waited for a response, Arnold began hearing some less than flattering opinions of his recent military action. Arnold had behaved rashly, some were saying. He cared only for personal glory—why else would a sane man pick a fight with the British navy? And in the end, all of the ships under his command had been lost. General William Maxwell summed up the critics' point of view: "Arnold, our evil genius to the north, has, with a good deal of industry, got us clear of all our fine fleet."

In Philadelphia, meanwhile, members of Congress

were getting sick of seeing American military leaders treated like celebrities. "I have been distressed," John Adams said, "to see some members of this house disposed to idolize an image which their own hands have molded." Adams was referring to George Washington, but his point applied to Arnold also. Military heroes, Adams argued, could easily overshadow less glamorous elected officials. And that would be the end of America's experiment with democracy.

While this was going on, Washington submitted a request to Congress for five new major generals—it was up to the members to choose which brigadier generals to promote. Here was a chance for Congress to show General Washington who was in charge.

Washington knew how sensitive congressmen were about their authority, and he was careful not to step on their toes. But he hoped they would at least take his suggestions when it came to fighting the war. They didn't.

Washington was scanning a newspaper in late February when he saw the article with the official announcement. Holding back his famous temper, he read that Congress had named the five major generals, and none of the men were ones he wanted. Worst of all, they'd passed over Benedict Arnold. "Surely a more active, a more spirited and sensible officer fills no department in your army," Washington complained privately to a friend in Congress.

This was a serious problem, and not just because Washington thought Arnold deserved the higher rank. Arnold had been first in line for promotion, ahead of the five men Congress chose. Washington knew Arnold well enough to know that Arnold would miss the bigger political picture and see this as a personal insult. He would feel obliged, as a man of honor, to resign.

"I beg you will not take any hasty steps," Washington wrote to Arnold. He suggested that perhaps Arnold was "omitted through some mistake." He promised to look into it right away.

"I am greatly obliged to Your Excellency for interesting yourself so much in my behalf," Arnold wrote back. "Congress, undoubtedly, have a right of promoting those whom, from their abilities, and their long and arduous services, they esteem most deserving. Their promotion of junior officers to the rank of major generals, I view as a very civil way of requesting my resignation, as unqualified for the office I hold."

As Washington had feared, the deeply offended Arnold said, "I can no longer serve my country with honor." He did, however, agree to give Washington some time. "I shall certainly avoid any hasty step that may tend to the injury of my country."

Finally, in April, there was another letter from Washington. Arnold had not been skipped over by mistake, Washington reported. "The point does not now admit of a doubt," he wrote, "and is of so delicate a nature that I will not even undertake to advise. Your own feelings must be your guide." Congress' choices, Washington explained, had been based on political considerations, rivalries between states and regions. "I confess it is a strange mode of reasoning," he commented, "but it may serve to show you, that the promotion, which was due to your seniority, was not overlooked for want of merit in you."

Arnold didn't buy that for a second. He suspected, correctly, that the stories told by enemies he'd made over the past two years were damaging his standing in Congress. "I know some villain has been busy with my fame, and busily slandering me," he said. "I cannot think of drawing my sword until my reputation, which is dearer than life, is cleared up."

Arnold also received bad news from Elizabeth DeBlois. "Miss DeBlois has positively refused to listen to the general," Lucy Knox said to her husband, "which, with his other mortifications, will come very hard upon him."

Lucy wrote to Arnold, saying that Betsy had returned the trunk of gowns and announced her intention to marry her sweetheart, a young apothecary's apprentice.

There was another note, this one from Henry Knox, asking if Lucy could keep one of the pretty scarves from the trunk. Arnold wrote back to Knox saying no, sorry, he needed everything in the trunk—he didn't give up that easily.

Arnold sat at home, besieged by his bitter enemies: idle time and politics. He could even feel an attack of gout settling on his legs.

The war saved him. At three in the morning on April 25, he was awakened by a militiaman pounding on the front door.

EXCEEDINGLY UNHAPPY
April 25–July 11, 1777

Standing outside Arnold's house in the pouring rain, the militiaman told Arnold that a large British force had landed on the Connecticut coast and was now slashing and burning its way toward the town of Danbury.

Arnold threw on his uniform, leaped onto his horse, and raced toward Danbury, thirty miles away. Militiamen from nearby towns were gathering as Arnold arrived. It was still dark, but the sky above the town glowed red, lit by dozens of burning buildings.

After sunrise the two-thousand-man British force began a twenty-mile march back to its ships on Long Island Sound. Arnold had about five hundred shivering, tired, frightened volunteers. He decided to attack.

Arranging his militia across the road the British

would have to use, Arnold rode back and forth in front of the line, telling the inexperienced men to stay calm and hold their fire until the enemy got closer.

But when the enemy did get closer, the Americans broke and scattered. Arnold was galloping along the road, urging the men to stand and fight, when he heard a series of sickening thuds and felt his horse collapsing beneath him. Shot nine times, the animal fell to the dirt, trapping Arnold's leg in the tangled stirrups.

A British soldier ran toward Arnold, pointing his bayonet, calling, "Surrender! You are my prisoner!"

"Not yet!" Arnold shouted, pulling his pistol from his belt and killing the soldier with a single shot.

Managing to yank his leg out of the stirrups, he scrambled to his feet and took off running across a swamp. Bullets buzzed all around Arnold—a couple actually went through his hat—as he leaped over a fence and sprinted into the woods.

Once again the British were impressed. After the Danbury action, a British intelligence report described Arnold as having "the character of a devilish fighting fellow."

When news of the Danbury fight reached Congress, members decided to reconsider their decision not to promote Arnold. "The ballots being taken," said John Adams, "Brigadier General Benedict Arnold was promoted to the rank of major general."

Washington sent his thanks to Congress, but pointed out a problem—since they'd been major generals longer, the five men promoted over Arnold's head still outranked him. "What shall be done about his rank?" Washington asked. "He will not act, most probably, under those he commanded but a few weeks ago."

He was right to be worried. Arnold still felt slighted, convinced that attacks on his character were at the root of what he saw as his disrespectful handling by Congress. And there certainly had been attacks on Arnold's character. Currently making the rounds in Philadelphia was a pamphlet written by John Brown, an old enemy from the Ethan Allen/Fort Ticonderoga days, and a close friend of James Easton—the man Arnold had kicked and beaten with his sword.

In early May, Arnold went to meet Washington at his headquarters in New Jersey. He showed Washington Brown's pamphlet, which accused Arnold of having a "character not worth a sixpence." Openly charging Arnold with stealing from the merchants of Montreal, Brown declared, "Money is this man's god, and to get enough of it, he would sacrifice his country."

That line infuriated Arnold. "Whenever I have an opportunity of seeing him," he said, "he shall no longer have reason to complain for want of satisfaction."

Washington urged Arnold to calm down—the last thing Arnold needed was to fight a public duel.

Arnold agreed to hold off on the gunplay. As an alternative, he announced, he would go to Philadelphia and convince Congress to restore his seniority. If that failed, he would have to resign.

Before Arnold left camp, Washington gave him a sealed letter to be handed to John Hancock, president of Congress. "It is needless to say anything of this gentleman's military character," Washington wrote. "It is universally known that he has always distinguished himself as a judicious, brave officer, of great activity, enterprise, and perseverance."

Washington watched Arnold ride off to Philadelphia. He must have known that no good could come of it.

Arnold made his case to Congress on May 19. Or, he tried to—his lack of political skill hurt him. What began as a sincere appeal for justice quickly turned into angry whining. "I am exceedingly unhappy," he told

Congress, "to find that after having made every sacrifice of fortune, ease and domestic happiness to serve my country, I am publicly impeached, in particular by Lt. Colonel Brown, of a catalogue of crimes, which, if true, ought to subject me to disgrace, infamy, and the just resentment of my countrymen."

Members of Congress responded with a vote of public thanks for Arnold's battlefield efforts, throwing in a new horse "as a token of their approbation of his gallant conduct in the action against the enemy in their late enterprise in Danbury."

Arnold was trying to restore his honor. He got a horse. Not quite the same thing.

He decided to stay in Philadelphia, where he spent his time lobbying key members of Congress. Again, this simply wasn't his strength. One particularly annoyed member referred to Arnold as "uninteresting and sometimes indelicate."

John Adams was kinder. "I spent last evening at the war office with General Arnold," Adams wrote to his wife, Abigail. "He has been basely slandered and libeled." But what Arnold just could not understand was that he was in the middle of a political fight. Alarmed by the growing power of George Washington and his generals, Congress was desperate to solidify civilian control over the military. Giving in to Arnold's request would set a dangerous precedent. Besides, Arnold wasn't the only general with hurt feelings. "I am wearied to death with the wrangling between military officers," Adams sighed. "They quarrel like cats and dogs . . . scrambling for rank and pay like apes for nuts."

The larger political issues meant nothing to Benedict Arnold—to Arnold, everything was personal. He hung around Philadelphia week after week, following members of Congress around, sucking up, making himself sick with the effort. He knew he was fighting a losing battle. But he was putting off facing his only other option: resignation from the army.

As he walked the streets, killing time, he watched the city prepare for a huge Fourth of July celebration—the first anniversary of the Declaration of Independence. He could feel people watching him. Although they greeted him warmly, it seemed to Arnold that everyone was waiting to see how the famous warrior would react to being publicly humiliated.

Finally, on July 10, he wrote his letter of resignation. "My feelings are deeply wounded," he told Congress. "It is not in my power to serve my country in the present rank I hold."

On July 11 he walked into the Pennsylvania State House, handed in the letter, walked back out, and stood in the street. What next? Back to his old life in New Haven? That didn't exist—his wife was dead, his business crippled by war. What next?

ARNOLD RIDES NORTH

July 11–August 24, 1777

❦

On the same day Arnold turned in his resignation, Congress got another letter, this one from General Washington. The British had begun their expected attack from Canada and were already driving across northern New York. If they made it to the Hudson River and sliced the United States in two, Washington warned, "the most disagreeable consequences may be apprehended." In other words, the Americans would lose the war.

The Northern Army needed help, and the commander knew the man he wanted to send. "If General Arnold has settled his affairs," wrote Washington, "and can be spared from Philadelphia, I would recommend him for this business, and that he should immediately set out for the northern department."

Breaking his own rule about not pestering Congress, Washington wrote again the next day with the exact same request. "I have thought it my duty to repeat my wishes on the subject, and that he may without a moment's loss of time, set out from Philadelphia."

Congress asked Arnold to set aside his resignation and hurry to Washington's headquarters for further orders. Arnold agreed. Both Congress and Arnold were glad to be rid of each other.

Arnold reached Washington's Hudson River headquarters on the night of July 17. Washington came out to shake his hand, and the men walked together to Washington's tent.

The situation was serious, Washington explained. It was basically a continuation of the British attack from 1776, but bigger. British General John Burgoyne had already taken Fort Ticonderoga, and his army was chopping its way across the forests on route to the Hudson River at Albany. If the British made it there, they could begin their plan of cutting the Colonies in two.

Washington needed to keep his main army where it was, to try to prevent the British army in New York City from moving south to Philadelphia. So he assigned

Arnold to rush to the Northern Army and help it prepare for a do-or-die stand against Burgoyne.

Arnold left Washington's camp, riding north through the night.

General Burgoyne was not exactly riding through the night. "Having a jolly time" is how Burgoyne spent his nights, according to one officer's wife who was traveling with the army. He was, she said, "spending half the night singing and drinking and amusing himself in the company of the wife of a commissary, who was his mistress and, like him, loved champagne."

Fun loving and cocky, Burgoyne had actually bet a friend in London he'd have the war won in under a year. Now he was about forty miles north of Albany, moving slowly but steadily toward his goal. The Americans were doing everything possible to block his progress—felling big trees across paths, destroying bridges, diverting streams to flood low-lying parts of the route—but Burgoyne was unconcerned. "The only purpose it can answer is to retard me for a time," he reported. "It cannot finally impede me."

In early August General Schuyler called the top Northern Army officers to a council of war. Arnold listened to

Schuyler describe the crisis: the army had about six thousand soldiers, but half the men were sick with colds or fevers. Burgoyne, with about eight thousand, was still advancing slowly. The Americans could not avoid a showdown for long. Meanwhile, a second British force, under Colonel Barry St. Leger, was coming at the Americans from the west. Leger had about 750 British regulars, plus a thousand Mohawk warriors—fierce fighters. They were now surrounding a small American force at Fort Stanwix. If they took that fort they would pour down the Mohawk River Valley toward Albany, putting the Northern Army in a deadly vise between St. Leger and Burgoyne.

Schuyler had to decide whether or not to divide his army and send part of it to Fort Stanwix. He asked his officers for their opinions. One by one, the men urged Schuyler not to divide the already outnumbered army. Then it was Arnold's turn. *Divide the army,* he said, *Fort Stanwix must not fall.*

Schuyler agreed with Arnold. He asked his officers who would lead the mission.

No one spoke.

Schuyler walked up and down the room, biting down hard on his pipe, his face turning deeper and deeper shades of red.

One of the officers mumbled, "He means to weaken the army."

Schuyler snapped the pipe between his teeth, turned toward the table, and said, "Gentlemen, I shall take the responsibility upon myself. Fort Stanwix and the Mohawk Valley shall be saved! Where is the brigadier who will command the relief?"

Arnold spoke up. He'd do it.

He quickly set out with nine hundred men. "Nothing shall be omitted that can be done to raise the siege [at Fort Stanwix]," he said. "You will hear of my being victorious, or no more."

Benedict Arnold neared Fort Stanwix on August 21, and scouts confirmed reports that the British force was twice the size of his. Arnold wanted to attack anyway, but the other officers voted to send for reinforcements. Arnold could overrule them, of course, but he didn't want to go into battle with reluctant officers.

While Arnold paced in the small cabin he was using for his headquarters, wondering what in the world he could do next, a woman shoved past the soldiers at the door and practically tumbled into the room, wailing like a wounded dog. She fell at Arnold's feet and grabbed his legs.

Arnold, irritated and confused, separated himself from the woman. Then a soldier stepped into the cabin and explained everything. The woman's son, a young man named Hon Yost, had been caught recruiting Loyalist soldiers to join the British attack. He'd just been tried, found guilty, condemned to death.

Arnold told the mother that there was nothing he could do. The man was a traitor. He deserved to die.

The mother tried to explain that Hon Yost didn't know any better, that he was just a friendly boy who talked too much. He was not too bright, she admitted, but he was harmless at heart. She urged Arnold to at least meet the boy, to judge for himself.

Arnold nodded, and soldiers brought Hon Yost in. He was big and sloppily dressed, but he had a sly grin on his face. Arnold thought he wasn't quite as slow as his mother claimed.

Arnold told Hon Yost to take off his coat. He had his soldiers take the coat outside and blast a few holes through it. He gave it back to Hon Yost and told him to put it back on. Then he told Hon Yost his plan. Later that day, Arnold watched the man disappear into the woods, heading toward Fort Stanwix.

☙

The next morning Hon Yost stumbled into St. Leger's camp. A group of Mohawks saw him first and aimed their weapons.

Pointing to the bullet holes in his coat, a hysterical Hon Yost explained that he'd barely escaped from the Americans. Benedict Arnold was on his way right now with a huge American army!

The Mohawks asked how many men Arnold had.

Hon Yost shrugged and gestured to the countless leaves on the trees above, as if to say, *That many!*

Dragged into St. Leger's tent, Hon Yost suddenly showed the ability to speak fairly well. Arnold was coming with two thousand troops, he said. They would arrive within twenty-four hours.

Outside St. Leger's tent was utter chaos. Sick of the siege, sick of being bossed around by the British, the Mohawks leaped at the excuse to take off—and to have some fun doing it. "You mean to sacrifice us!" they shouted as they ran around camp, laughing, firing guns, waving tomahawks, and grabbing supplies.

Many of St. Leger's soldiers panicked, tossed away packs and tents, and took off into the woods. St. Leger had no choice but to retreat. The army was next seen at Lake Ontario, seventy miles away.

Arnold arrived at Fort Stanwix on August 24. The

Americans in the fort came out and told him the British were gone—they'd just disappeared.

Arnold reported the news to Northern Army headquarters: "Nothing to be feared from the enemy in this quarter at present."

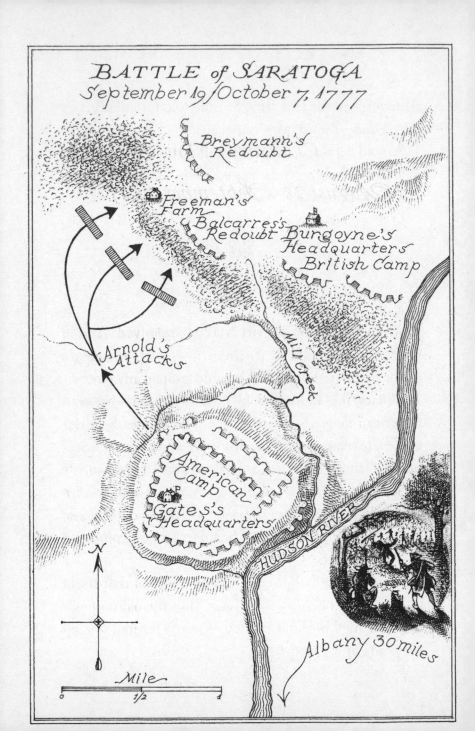

BATTLE of SARATOGA
September 19/October 7, 1777

Breymann's
Redoubt

Freeman's
Farm

Balcarres's
Redoubt
Burgoyne's
Headquarters
British Camp

Arnold's
Attacks

Mill Creek

American
Camp
Gates's
Headquarters

HUDSON RIVER

N

Albany 30 miles

Mile
0   1/2   1

CONQUER OR DIE
August 28–September 20, 1777

With the situation at Fort Stanwix resolved, Arnold hurried back to the Northern Army camp, knowing a major battle with the British could happen any day.

In fact the fighting had already started—between American generals, that is. The old enemies Schuyler and Gates had spent the past year wrestling for command of the Northern Army. Gates finally won, mostly because Congress had to blame someone for the recent fall of Fort Ticonderoga, and they decided to blame Schuyler. Congress ordered Schuyler to turn command over to Gates.

It was an icy hand-over. "I have done all that could be done," said Schuyler to Gates, "but the palm of victory is denied me, and it is left to you, General, to reap the fruits of my labors."

STEVE SHEINKIN

For Horatio Gates, it was the opportunity of a lifetime. Born in Britain, Gates was the illegitimate son of
a duke and the duke's housekeeper. As a young man he
had joined the British army, discovered that he couldn't
get far in that insider's world, and moved to America to
try his luck. Now, at the age of fifty, he finally saw
his chance to break through and achieve glory. Taking
over from Schuyler, Gates commanded a big American
army, with a massive battle coming—a battle that could
determine the outcome of the war. Nothing could get
in his way.

Then, riding back into camp, came Benedict Arnold.

On September 12 the Americans started digging in
along a string of hills stretching west from the Hudson
River, near the town of Saratoga. They chopped trenches
and threw up simple forts, just walls of earth and wood.
As the British marched closer, volunteers poured into
the American camp. The army was getting stronger
every day.

Gates and Arnold had gotten along fairly well until
this point. But when Gates wrote to Congress describing the British retreat from Fort Stanwix, he added no
mention of Arnold, no note of thanks. Arnold offended

Gates right back, filling his personal staff with officers who'd been on Schuyler's staff.

But their feud went beyond the personal—the men had a fundamental disagreement over how to fight the coming battle. Gates well remembered Arnold's performance at Valcour Island. He had been brave, but too aggressive, borderline reckless. No need for such heroics in the coming battle, Gates believed. The American army was in an excellent defensive position. Let the British march up to our forts; let them smash themselves against our walls.

Arnold saw things differently. To him, this was a continuation of the back-and-forth battle he'd begun in 1775—the Lake Champlain forts, Quebec, Valcour Island, and now the decisive round to come at Saratoga. Many veterans of the earlier campaigns were at Saratoga, including Daniel Morgan and his riflemen. They were ready to finish the job—*their* job. Arnold summed up his strategy like this: "We ought to march out and attack them." Prevent the British from using their well-practiced battle formations, Arnold argued. Force them to fight in the woods, disrupt their plans, create chaos.

Gates got so sick of this argument that he stopped

inviting Arnold to his strategy meetings. Henry Livingston, one of Arnold's new aides, reported: "I have for some time past observed the great coolness, and in many instances, even disrespect, with which General Arnold has been treated at Headquarters."

By the morning of September 19, the British were close, so close that American soldiers could hear the pounding of British drums. Then, as the sun burned off the fog, Americans caught the glint of sunlight bouncing off British weapons in the fields and woods ahead.

Gates told his officers to let them come.

It was exactly what Burgoyne was counting on—his battle plan was based on the guess that Gates would be cautious and fight from behind the walls of the fort. The British rolled their cannon toward the forts, and opened fire at 10:00 a.m.

As the bombs began falling, Arnold rode to Gates's tent. Richard Varick, another of Arnold's young aides, said that Arnold "urged, begged, and entreated" Gates not to let the British get any closer. Finally, just to shut Arnold up, Gates agreed to let Arnold take out about two thousand troops.

An American officer named Alexander Scammell described what happened next: "Arnold rushed into the thickest of the fight with his usual recklessness, and at times acted like a madman."

"Nothing could exceed the bravery of Arnold on this day," remembered Captain Ebenezer Wakefield, "he seemed the very genius of war."

Arnold led his men toward the gunfire, crashing into the British in the twelve-acre field of a local farmer named John Freeman. After getting blown backward by British fire, Daniel Morgan and his riflemen climbed trees around the field, lay in the branches, and picked off British officers.

The two forces drove each other back and forth across Freeman's stump-covered farm all afternoon. "Both armies seemed determined to conquer or die," said the American general John Glover.

The thunder of gunfire bounced off the thick forests surrounding the field, adding to the roar of battle. "Such an explosion of fire I never had any idea of before," said a British officer.

Alexander Scammell agreed, describing it as "the hottest fire of cannon and musketry that ever I heard in my life."

"For upwards of three hours the blaze from the artillery and small arms was incessant, and sounded like the roll of a drum," said Enoch Poor, an American general.

"By turns the British and Americans drove each other, taking and retaking the field, and often mingling in a hand-to-hand wrestle and fight."

Arnold charged around the field on his huge black stallion, Warren, shouting, "Come on, boys. Hurry up, my brave boys!"

"There seemed to shoot out from him a magnetic flame," Scammell said. "Riding in front of the line, his eyes flashing, pointing with his sword to the advancing foe, with a voice that rung clear as a trumpet and electrified the line, he called upon the men to follow him to the charge."

Sensing the chance for a knockout, Arnold sent message after message back to Gates, calling for reinforcements.

Gates stood outside his tent safely behind the fort's walls, chatting with his staff, listening to the battle, and following the updates brought back by soldiers. He got the messages from Arnold, but refused to release more troops, saying it was too risky.

Finally Arnold himself rode up on his stallion and jumped off in front of Gates. He begged Gates for more soldiers. Gates said no. Arnold pleaded and insisted. Finally, Gates agreed to send out a few hundred more men.

Just then an officer named Morgan Lewis rode up to report that the fight was still going back and forth, there was still no winner.

Arnold leaped back on his horse shouting, "By God, I will soon put an end to it!"

Gates watched him ride off. He and Lewis looked at each other. "You had better order him back," Lewis said. "He may, by some rash act, do mischief."

"I was instantly dispatched, overtook, and remanded Arnold to camp," remembered one of Gates's staff officers.

Arnold came back, but was furious about it. Standing outside his own tent, he watched the sun set and heard the sounds of gunfire die down, then stop.

The American fighters fell back behind their defensive lines, leaving Burgoyne in control of Freeman's field. This gave Burgoyne the right to claim victory, which, of course, he did. But the casualty figures told a different story: he had more than six hundred killed and wounded, to about three hundred for the Americans.

Wounded men lay all over the battlefield, calling out for help, crying for a drink of water. Frightened of being out in the open with American sharpshooters nearby, British burial parties quickly dug pits and dumped in the dead, leaving arms, legs, and even heads above ground. Wolves feasted that night on the dead and the dying.

In Burgoyne's headquarters, officers were trying to figure out what had gone wrong. Burgoyne's theory was this: "Arnold chose to give rather than receive the attack." Convinced the Americans wouldn't have the nerve or skill to fight him in the open, Burgoyne had been counting on rolling his big guns right up the American forts—and it should have worked. If only the Americans had followed Gates's original plan, Burgoyne lamented, "I should in a few hours have gained a position, that in spite of the enemy's numbers, would have put them in my power."

Gates was satisfied with the day's events. "The enemy suffered extremely in every quarter where they were engaged," he reported.

His position was now stronger than ever. The British had been mauled; many of their best officers had been killed. Burgoyne would have to throw his weakened forces against the American forts soon, or head back to Canada with his pompous British tail between his legs. Everything was working out beautifully.

BLOODY PIECE OF WORK

September 1777

Burgoyne was in a dangerous spot at Saratoga, but he was expecting help from New York City. According to his grand plans for the year, a major British force, under the command of General William Howe, was supposed to come up the Hudson River and threaten the Northern Army from behind. But Howe did not arrive. He hated Burgoyne and outranked him, too. So, rather than playing a supporting role in Burgoyne's drama, Howe decided to capture the American capital of Philadelphia.

John André, still in New York, heard the army was heading into combat. He wrote out his will, leaving his money to his younger brother and three sisters. Then he headed south with Howe to attack George Washington.

On September 20, just one day after Arnold's big

battle at Saratoga, André prepared for battle himself. General Grey, André's new boss, explained the mission. They were going to attack an American army camp near Paoli, Pennsylvania. They were going to do it at night, and without guns.

André went from company to company, telling men to take the flints out of their muskets; they would use bayonets only. Grey wanted to surprise the sleeping Americans, and he wanted to send them a grisly message about the price of rebellion.

The British soldiers marched through a dark forest, guided by the distant light of campfires. Just after midnight, reported André, they charged into the American camp, "putting to the bayonet all they came up with." Americans jumped up, screaming, panicking. All around André could hear the sounds of steel blades plunging through flesh, and the cries of dying men. "It was a most bloody piece of work," he said, "and I believe, will alarm them very much."

Grey's men went on thrusting and slicing, even after the Americans tried to surrender. "I with my own eyes, see them cut and hack some of our poor men to pieces after they had fallen on their hands," said one survivor. When a doctor examined the dead he found one with forty-six stab wounds.

☙

At least two hundred Americans were killed in what became known as the Paoli Massacre. Grey's midnight attack helped open the road for the British to march to Philadelphia. Members of Congress packed up quickly and scurried out of town.

As the British marched toward the capital, André was convinced the war was just about won. And he was pretty pleased with his own performance, which, as he reported to his mother, drew praise from General Grey. "I must be vain enough to tell you that he seemed satisfied with my assistance on that occasion, and that he thanked me in the warmest terms."

BEYOND RECONCILIATION
September 20–October 7, 1777

❧

Washington's losses near Philadelphia intensified the pressure on the Northern Army to stop the British advance in New York. And the mood in the American camp was tense enough already. As one officer put it, "Generals Gates and Arnold have differed beyond reconciliation."

Reporting to Congress on the recent battle at Saratoga, Gates wrote, "the general good behavior of the troops on this important occasion cannot be surpassed by the most veteran army." Contrary to all military tradition, though, he made no mention of the leading role Benedict Arnold and his division played in the day's success.

Arnold was stunned and insulted. And that was before he read the new order from Gates's headquarters: "Colonel Morgan's corps," directed Gates, "is to make returns and reports to headquarters only, from whence alone he is to receive orders."

Gates was removing Daniel Morgan from Arnold's division of the army, crippling Arnold's ability to take the initiative in battle. This made no sense militarily, since Arnold and Morgan fought so effectively together. But it made perfect sense to Gates, who had two worries about the coming fight with Burgoyne. The first: Arnold might do something crazy and cause the Americans to lose. The second: Arnold might do something crazy, win the battle—and get the credit. Gates found neither option acceptable.

Arnold worked himself into a fury in his tent, then charged across camp and barreled into Gates's hut, nearly knocking down Gates's aide James Wilkinson on the way in.

"Matters were altercated in a very high strain," said Arnold's aide Livingston, who tagged along to watch. "Both were warm," he said, adding that Gates was "rather passionate and very assuming."

Arnold was "in great warmth," Wilkinson recalled. "High words and gross language ensued."

Oh, to know exactly what that gross language was! We don't—but we know that they fought over credit for the battle of September 19, and over who should command Daniel Morgan and his men. We know Gates remained a bit cooler than Arnold, sitting at his desk while Arnold paced. When Arnold demanded the respect due to a man in his position in the army, Gates needled his opponent expertly.

"I don't know of you being a major general," Gates said, calmly pushing up the glasses that were constantly sliding down his long nose. "You sent in your resignation to Congress."

"Arnold's spirit could not brook this usage," said Livingston.

Seeing this, Gates jabbed the needle again, telling Arnold that Major General Benjamin Lincoln—one of the men promoted over Arnold's head—was on his way to camp. When Lincoln arrived, Arnold would no longer be needed, and could leave whenever he wished.

At this point, Wilkinson said, "Arnold retired in a rage." Arnold strode back toward his tent, waving his arms and calling his commander "the face of clay," and several other things.

Back in his tent, Arnold calmed down just enough to hold a pen. "I have been received with the greatest coolness at headquarters," he complained to Gates, "and often huffed in such a manner as must mortify a person with less pride than I have."

Gates's reply pushed Arnold closer to the edge: "I know not what you mean by insult or indignity."

Arnold tumbled into Gates's trap, demanding a pass to go to Pennsylvania. "Where I propose to join General Washington," he wrote, "and may possibly have it in my power to serve my country, although I am thought of no consequence in this department."

Gates gladly sent the pass.

But Arnold didn't leave Saratoga. Still in camp on September 24, Arnold watched General Lincoln arrive and thought he saw Lincoln giving orders to his—Arnold's—wing of the army. Arnold charged out of his tent, shouting vows of "certain death" to anyone who tried to command his men.

The next day Gates issued new orders. Lincoln was now in charge of what had been Arnold's wing. If Arnold interfered again, he would be arrested.

"I have reason to think your treatment proceeds from a spirit of jealousy," Arnold wrote to Gates. Then, displaying his typical touch for diplomacy, he went on to give Gates military advice.

Gates sent back a note saying basically, *Oh, are you still here?*

It was awkward and embarrassing for Arnold to stay at Saratoga, but he just couldn't leave—not with the most important battle of the Revolution coming any day.

By early October, frost covered the grass in the mornings. The leaves on the trees glowed yellow and red in the sunlight. Volunteers continued pouring into the American camp. Gates now had about ten thousand men to Burgoyne's five thousand.

The British were still camped in front of the American lines, but they couldn't stay there much longer. "From the best intelligence," Gates said of Burgoyne, "he has not more than three week's provisions in store."

All day sharpshooters fired deadly rounds into each other's camp. At night wolves came out of the woods and dug up shallow graves between the armies. "They were similar to a pack of hounds," said one British soldier, "for one setting up a cry, they all joined and, when they approached a corpse, their noise was hideous until they had scratched it up."

On October 7 scouts brought Gates news: the British were on the move. Gates sent Wilkinson out to take a look. "I perceived about half a mile from the line of our encampment several columns of the enemy," he said. "I returned and reported to the general, who asked me what appeared to be the intentions of the enemy."

"I think, sir, they offer you battle," Wilkinson told Gates.

"And what is your opinion?" asked Gates.

"I would indulge them."

Gates nodded. "Well, then, order Morgan on to begin the game."

Arnold stood in front of his tent, listening to the gunfire. It was getting louder, more intense. He rushed to Gates's cabin and asked permission to ride out toward the British—just to see what was happening.

Gates hesitated, then said, "I am afraid to trust you, Arnold."

Arnold hung around, listening to Gates give orders for a small number of soldiers to advance.

"That is nothing," Arnold cut in. "You must send a stronger force."

"General Arnold," snapped Gates, "I have nothing for you to do. You have no business here."

As Arnold walked back toward his tent, he watched his old comrades Daniel Morgan and Henry Dearborn leading their men out to the fight. To Arnold, those were his men, and this was his battle. Arnold jumped on his black stallion, and, Wilkinson remembered, he "rode about the camp betraying great agitation and wrath."

The explosions grew louder. Gunpowder clouds began rising above the trees. Arnold looked over at Gates's headquarters, where Gates stood, looking calm, talking with the officers who raced up with updates.

Arnold couldn't stand it another second. "No man shall keep me in my tent today!" he shouted. "Victory or death!"

Gates looked up from his conversation just in time to see Arnold jab his spurs into his horse and charge toward the battlefield. He ordered an aide to ride after Arnold and bring him back.

Soldiers cheered when they saw Arnold coming.

"What regiment is this?" Arnold asked the men.

"Colonel Latimer's, sir."

"God bless you! I am glad to see you," said Arnold. "Now come on, boys. If the day is long enough, we'll have them all in hell before night!"

This was another day of chaotic combat, just how Arnold liked it. Men dragged small cannon on wheeled carriages through the woods and fields. They blasted at each other from behind bushes, trees, farm buildings, and the low walls of their log forts. Arnold was all over the place, yelling for men to follow him, wildly waving his sword. At one point he accidently hit one of his own men on the head—the soldier was fine, though he later asked for an apology, which Arnold gave.

"He was found on the field of battle exercising command, but not by the order or permission of General Gates," Wilkinson said of Arnold. "His conduct was exceedingly rash and intemperate; and he exposed himself with great folly and temerity."

The British army's position was anchored by two key forts, the Balcarres Redoubt and the Breymann Redoubt, each named for the officer in command. Take one of these forts, and the Americans could flank the enemy, ride right around them and attack them from the rear.

Gates had not wanted to risk attacking the British once they fell back into these forts—but Gates was no longer in control. Arnold led charge after charge at the Balcarres Redoubt, hurling himself and his men into a storm of British musket fire and grapeshot. Forced to fall back to the trees, Arnold looked across the battlefield and realized he was attacking the wrong fort—the Breymann Redoubt was the weaker spot. Then he did something extreme, even by Arnold's standards.

"He dashed to the left through the fire of the two

lines," Wilkinson said. Rather than take the time to ride around the fighting, Arnold rode between the opposing armies, somehow dodging bullets for 120 yards, reaching the Americans in front of the Breymann Redoubt.

"He behaved, as I then thought, more like a madman than a cool and discreet officer," one officer remarked.

Arnold collected a small group of soldiers and led the charge on the Breymann Redoubt. Breymann's men fired their guns and cannons, blasting several American heads and arms into the air. Arnold regrouped his force and attacked again.

There was another blast, and another sheet of metal exploded out from the redoubt. Arnold felt a bullet slice through his left leg as his horse collapsed underneath him. His wounded leg hit the ground first and splintered under the weight of the falling horse.

"Rush on, my brave boys, rush on!" he shouted from the ground.

Enemy soldiers broke and ran as Arnold's men scrambled up and over the walls of the Breymann Redoubt. From the ground, his shattered leg still trapped under his dead horse, Arnold watched the decisive victory he'd been struggling toward for three years.

A few of Arnold's men rushed to him and pulled him out from under his horse. They slung a blanket between two poles and gently lifted Arnold onto the stretcher. As the sun began to set, they carried him back toward camp.

It was at this point that Gates's messenger finally caught up with Arnold and passed on the commander's orders: Arnold was to return to camp before doing "some rash thing."

Arnold gritted his teeth to fight back the pain.

Henry Dearborn put a hand on Arnold's shoulder, asking, "Where are you hit?"

"In the same leg," Arnold said. "I wish it had been my heart."

FRACTURE BOX

October 8, 1777–January 20, 1778

❦

"The brave General Arnold is badly wounded in his left leg," reported a Connecticut newspaper, "having received a compound fracture, which endangers the loss of the limb."

Arnold was loaded into a wagon and endured a torturous ride to Albany. Every bump in the road caused the jagged edges of his broken bones to stab the nerves and torn flesh of his open wound. When he finally made it to the military hospital in Albany, doctors told him the leg would have to come off immediately. Arnold angrily dismissed the idea as "damned nonsense."

The doctors did the only thing they knew to do. They immobilized Arnold's leg inside a tight wooden frame, a "fracture box," they called it. They told Arnold he'd have to lie on his back for several months—and hope for the best.

Dr. James Thacher reported that Arnold was not pleased with his situation. "I watched with the celebrated General Arnold, whose leg was badly fractured by a musket ball," Thacher wrote in his journal. "He is very peevish and impatient under his misfortunes, and required all my attention during the night."

When he wasn't cursing his doctors, Arnold was following the news from Saratoga. After the crushing defeat of October 7, Burgoyne's army limped north, hoping somehow to make it back to Canada. Outnumbered three to one, nearly out of food, Burgoyne's force was quickly surrounded by Gates's men and forced to surrender.

On October 17, a total of 5,791 British soldiers and their German allies laid down their arms—by far the biggest event of the Revolution so far. Unable to believe they'd been beaten by a mob of country bumpkins, British soldiers smashed their muskets to the ground in front of the Americans. Drummers kicked holes in the skins of their drums as they set them down.

Burgoyne himself behaved with a bit more poise, walking up to Gates, taking off his hat, bowing, and saying, "The fortunes of war, General, have made me your prisoner."

Gates had his reply ready. "I shall always be glad to testify that it was through no fault of your Excellency."

Burgoyne then drew his sword and handed it to Gates. Gates held it for a few seconds, relished the feel of it, then handed it back. After this polite little ceremony, Gates led the way into his cabin, where two planks had been laid over empty beef barrels. On this rough table plates were piled with ham, goose, roast beef, and pitchers of rum and water.

Gates called on Burgoyne to make a toast. Burgoyne seemed unsure what to say, but finally raised his glass and said, "General Washington!"

Gates lifted his glass and offered, "King George!"

Privately, Gates was somewhat less courteous. "If Old England is not by this lesson taught humility," he said, "then she is an obstinate old slut, bent upon her ruin."

Arnold must have trembled with rage as he listened to these reports. Employing a great eighteenth-century term for coward, he declared Gates to be "the greatest poltroon in the world."

There was no word from Gates, no note of thanks to Arnold, or inquiry about his health. But there was plenty of news *about* Gates. Congress voted to strike a special medal just for the hero of Saratoga, awarding it to Gates with the resolution, "Your name, sir, will be written in the breasts of the grateful Americans and sent down to posterity." Arnold also heard that members of Congress and their wives were learning a new dance called "the Burgoyne Surrender."

Once again, idleness plagued Arnold. Flat on his back, his ruined leg nailed into a box, Arnold could do nothing but imagine over and over the beaming faces of congressmen as they handed Gates his medal, the smile on Gates's face as he graciously took credit for the American victory at Saratoga.

The images tormenting Arnold were clearly affecting his mood. "His peevishness would degrade the most capricious of the fair sex," complained one of his doctors. "He abuses us as a set of ignorant pretenders."

Finally, in mid-December, Arnold got some news about himself. Congress had voted to restore his seniority, ranking him once again ahead of the five generals who'd been promoted ahead of him ten months earlier. "General Arnold is restored to a violated right," Washington said when he heard the news.

Arnold didn't feel restored. Congress made no mention of Arnold's role in the victory at Saratoga, making the promotion sound like nothing more than a routine change in policy.

In late January 1778, Washington sent his personal congratulations. "May I venture to ask whether you are upon your legs again?" wrote Washington. "If you are not, may I flatter myself that you will be soon? There is none who wishes more sincerely for this event than I do, or who will receive the information with more pleasure."

Arnold was definitely not on his legs yet. The muscle damage in his left leg was so severe that it shrank as it healed, leaving it two inches shorter than the right leg.

"As soon as your situation will permit," continued Washington, "I request that you will repair to this army, it being my earnest wish to have your services in the ensuing campaign."

But the doctors were not even sure Arnold would walk again, let alone charge around on a warhorse. He had no idea if he'd ever be able to lead men into battle.

Or, if he'd want to.

PEGGY SHIPPEN

November 1777–April 1778

While Arnold lay in his Albany fracture box, John André marched triumphantly into Philadelphia with the British army.

Many Patriots had fled as the British arrived, leaving behind empty houses, which British officers quickly occupied. André and the rest of General Grey's staff moved into Benjamin Franklin's home, where André was delighted to find the best private library in the city. "I believe I shall be in a very quiet station henceforth," he wrote to his mother. "The only hardships I endure are being obliged to sleep in my bed, to sit down to a very good dinner every day, to gossip in Philadelphia, or to consider something fashionable to make me irresistible this winter."

Delighted to be back in a big city, British officers set up restaurants and clubs, cockfights in the alleys and elegant balls in the taverns. André found an abandoned theater and went right to work, sweeping out the cobwebs, building sets, and painting scenery—everyone was especially impressed with his landscapes. Naming the new theater company Howe's Thespians, in honor of their commanding general, André and friends put on thirteen different plays that winter. André himself took on a number of minor rolls; critics called him "a poor actor." André's plays were so popular, the theater had to send out a special notice asking officers to stop bribing the doorkeepers for extra tickets.

And then there were the women. British officers had heard of the famously lovely ladies of Philadelphia, and they were not disappointed. André enjoyed visiting young women in their family homes, playing his flute, reciting poetry, sketching the girls, charming everyone. Wherever he went he heard stories of a young lady named Peggy Shippen. One officer told him she was the best looking woman in America. "We were all in love with her," added another.

André remembered Peggy—he'd met her when he passed through town as a prisoner two years before. He decided to go introduce himself at the Shippen mansion.

ᴄᴏ

Peggy Shippen was eighteen. She was small, almost delicate-looking, with an intelligent face and attentive, gray-blue eyes. She was very pretty, friends said, but not vain about it. She had a serious streak, often puzzling people by passing up parties to stay home with her father, a prominent judge. She liked to read his books, to talk with him about politics, business, whatever he was working on.

André was intrigued. He spent long afternoons in the Shippen's sitting room, drinking tea, entertaining Peggy with his drawing, his music, and tales of his travels. He listened to her stories, too.

The Revolution had seemed exciting to Peggy at first. Soon after the war started, George Washington had come over and dined with the family. "Nobody in America could revere his character more than I did," Peggy said.

But the fighting had dragged on, threatening her hometown, and even her family. Her father, torn between loyalty to Britain and America, wishing only for the return of peace, tried to remain neutral. This made him suspect to the leaders of Pennsylvania, who put him on a list of citizens to watch. Judge Shippen lived in constant fear that a mob would come and drag him off—Peggy saw panic in his eyes any time there was a knock on the door.

When the opposing armies began battling for Philadelphia, Peggy had helped pack her family's plates into barrels. They loaded the barrels and some furniture into a wagon and fled to a farm in New Jersey. Peggy was stuck in the isolated farmhouse, bored to death, forbidden even to walk to nearby friends' houses for fear of the angry gangs that attacked suspected Loyalists, or anyone who looked rich.

One day Peggy heard drums beating, then fists banging on the door. Her father opened the door, and there stood a group of filthy men, proclaiming themselves to be the town's militia, producing an arrest warrant for Judge Shippen. Peggy listened, terrified and crying, as her father pleaded with the men. Finally they agreed to let him stay in the house—but he must not even step outside, they warned.

"The country will be laid waste by the two contending parties," wailed Judge Shippen. "In this dreadful situation, I am at a loss to know how to dispose of my family."

The British army had solved the problem by conquering Philadelphia. That made it safe for Peggy and her family to come back home.

John André and Peggy Shippen were seen together often at dances and plays that winter. On cold clear nights André and his friends would drive up in a sleigh piled high with carpets. Peggy and her older sisters jumped in, climbed under the carpets, and the whole crew spent the night singing and laughing and speeding up and down the frozen Delaware River.

All the while Washington's army was camped just twenty-five miles away, freezing and starving at Valley Forge. They were an easy target, but General William Howe showed no interest in leaving the comforts of town. One possible reason can be found in the lyrics of a song that was popular among British soldiers that winter:

> *"Sir William, he, snug as a flea,*
> *Lay all this time a-snoring;*
> *Nor dreamed of harm as he lay warm*
> *In bed with Mrs. Loring."*

Early in 1778, Howe was called back to London, where war planners were eager to know why he was spending so much time indoors. As a tribute to the commander who'd helped to advance his career, André decided to throw Howe the biggest party Philadelphia had ever seen.

BACK TO PHILADELPHIA
April 1–June 19, 1778

❧

After five months in his Albany hospital bed, Arnold was finally able to get up and hobble a few feet on a crutch. In the spring, he was placed on a stretcher and loaded into a wagon for the long ride home to Connecticut. The bumpy roads caused him so much pain that he had to stop often to rest. At one roadside inn, the men carrying his stretcher were forced to rip out part of the door frame to get him inside.

This was a gloomy, lonely time for Arnold, and his mind, when it wasn't plagued by thoughts of Gates and Congress, turned to the more pleasant subject of Betsy DeBlois. When he heard that Betsy's engagement to the apothecary's apprentice had fallen through, Arnold decided to try again.

"Twenty times I have taken up my pen to write to

you," he began, "and, as often has my trembling hand refused to obey the dictates of my heart." He had tried to forget her, he explained, with no success. "Neither time, absence, misfortunes, nor your cruel indifference have been able to efface the deep impressions your charms have made."

Betsy's response has been lost, but the gist of her note is reflected in Arnold's second letter. "Pardon me, dear Betsy, if I called you cruel," wrote Arnold. "Had I imagined my letter would have occasioned you a moment's uneasiness, I never should forgive myself for writing it." He refers to her request that he write to her no more, promising to obey her wishes. "Forget there is so unhappy a wretch, for let me perish if I would give you one moment's pain."

And that was the end of that.

Arnold continued his journey home. On May 4 he arrived in New Haven, greeted by the biggest hero's welcome the town had ever given. Crowds lined the streets, fife and drum bands played; militiamen fired a thirteen cannon salute. All the leading citizens were there, Arnold saw, even the governor. The people paraded along with his wagon, cheering Arnold all the way to his house on Water Street.

෴

Two weeks later crowds lined the waterfront in Philadelphia, joining a very different sort of celebration. May 18 was the day of John André's *Meschianza*—an Italian word meaning mixture, or, as André called it, "a variety of entertainments."

After months of preparation, André's all-day party kicked off with a parade on the river—decorated boats floating past cheering crowds, colorful flags flapping, cannon booming. "The music," André said, "the number of spectators and the brilliancy of the gay tribe which peopled the river made the whole uncommonly solemn and striking."

Next came a spectacular tournament of knights. Fourteen young officers, wearing brightly colored costumes designed by André, divided into opposing teams of seven: the Knights of the Burning Mountain vs. the Knights of the Blended Rose. André fought on the side of the Burning Mountain, wearing baggy pants, puffy pink sleeves, flowing hair ribbons, and holding a shield hand-painted with his own personal motto: "No rival."

Watching the action from a specially built pavilion were fourteen young maidens, decked out in outrageous André-designed Turkish princess outfits. The women, André explained, were "selected from the foremost in youth, beauty and fashion." Peggy Shippen, of course, was included.

Mounted on decorated horses, each knight rode past the pavilion, saluted his lady, and then lined up to fight. A knight from one team rode forward and pronounced, "The Knights of the Blended Rose, by me their herald, proclaim and assert that the Ladies of the Blended Rose excel in wit, beauty, and every accomplishment, those of the whole world."

An opposing knight took exception, declaring, "The Knights of the Burning Mountain present themselves here, not to contest by words, but to disprove by deeds, the vain-glorious assertions of the Knights of the Blended Rose."

Trumpets sounded and squires handed the knights their lances. The knights rode toward each other, did a little fake jousting, got down from the horses, did a little fake dueling with swords, then strode to their ladies and kneeled down before them.

After dark the whole party moved to a waterfront mansion for a massive meal, fireworks, and dancing until dawn. All in all, André felt he'd pulled off "the most splendid entertainment, I believe, ever given by an army to their General."

Peggy's friend Becky Franks agreed, saying, "We

never had, and perhaps never shall have, so elegant an entertainment in America again."

Three days after the *Meschianza*, Arnold's carriage rolled into Valley Forge, coming to a stop in the mud in front of Washington's headquarters. Four soldiers helped Arnold down from the carriage. A fifth handed him his crutches.

Inside the cabin, with his weak leg up on a stool, Arnold listened to Washington review the nightmare winter his army had endured. More than two thousand men had died of disease, hunger, and cold, and Washington was furious with Congress for its inability to supply his army. But there was some good news. After months of effort in Paris, Benjamin Franklin had finally secured an alliance between the United States and France. It was the stunning American victory at Saratoga that had convinced the French that the Americans could actually win the war, persuading them to sign.

Then the conversation moved on to Arnold's future role in the army. Washington saw that Arnold couldn't ride yet, which meant he couldn't lead men in the field. But Washington's spies were telling him that the British were planning to pull out of Philadelphia. Washington would need someone in the capital city, a military governor, someone he could trust to restore order and keep the British away.

The assignment called for a delicate touch, given how sensitive Congress was about its authority, how wary of popular military leaders. And Pennsylvania's state leaders, who also met in Philadelphia, were just as prickly, maybe worse. Then there were all of the citizens in town who were trying to remain neutral—like it or not, they'd have to be protected from retribution by angry Patriots. This was a job that would require the ability to balance a confusing mix of cross-firing factions; it would call for patience, tact, and political skill.

For reasons no one has ever been able to figure out, Washington offered the job to Benedict Arnold.

Washington's spies were right, the British were planning to evacuate Philadelphia. The city was of little strategic value to the British—they'd be better off back in New York City, which was a better port, more defensible, and a stronger base for future operations.

British soldiers opened the jails, letting everyone out. Then they began removing their artillery from fortifications around the city. On June 17, as temperatures soared toward 100 degrees, soldiers and Loyalists ran in and out of houses and shops, packing crates and wagons.

The whole city, said one soldier, "greatly resembled a fair on the last day of business."

At Ben Franklin's house, André was doing some packing of his own, loading cases with Franklin's books, china, and musical instruments. "Captain André also took with him the picture of you, which hung in the dining room," Franklin's daughter wrote to her father after arriving a few days later.

André had just enough time to dash off a poem for the women of Philadelphia:

> *If at the close of war and strife*
> *My destiny once more,*
> *Should in the varied paths of life*
> *Conduct me to your shore. . . .*

> *Say! Wilt thou then receive again,*
> *And welcome to thy sight,*
> *The youth who bids with stifled pain*
> *His sad farewell tonight?*

André snipped off a lock of his hair and gave it to Peggy Shippen. Then he loaded his loot onto a wagon and rode off.

The next day thousands of people came out to cheer the American army as it marched back into Philadelphia. Cannon boomed and church bells clanged all over the city. Sitting in the center of the parade, wearing a new blue uniform with buff trim and gold buttons, his left leg propped up on the seat of his carriage, rode the new military governor of Philadelphia. Benedict Arnold smiled and waved to the cheering crowds.

CUPID'S WOUND
June 20–September 14, 1778

❦

The whole city stank. The British had left behind piles of rotting garbage, decaying horse corpses, and mass graves piled with the bodies of American prisoners of war who had died during the occupation. Houses and fences had been taken apart for firewood, windows smashed, churches used as stables and left uncleaned. As people poured back into town to see what was left of their homes and businesses, the streets jammed up with traffic, and drivers shouted and cursed each other.

In the midst of this chaos, Congress wanted a complete inventory of all the goods in the city. The goal was to figure out what belonged to whom, and to determine which of the goods left behind by the British and

Loyalists might be useful to the army. Following these orders, Arnold sent his soldiers out to padlock the doors of stores and warehouses. The city was shut down.

George Washington had offered Arnold some last-minute advice about his new job: "Adopt such measures as shall appear to you most effectual, and at the same time least offensive."

But as Washington really should have anticipated, Arnold began offending immediately. He settled in the elegant Penn mansion, the same building in which General Howe had just spent the winter. He posted uniformed guards outside the door, bought expensive new furniture, hired cooks, maids, and coachmen, and rode around town in a stylish new carriage.

This was an irritating display of luxury to a suffering city. Angry merchants and shop owners started coming over, complaining that Arnold had locked them out of their stores. Arnold explained that he was trying to restore order, and was just following orders from Congress. But he was rude to his visitors, dismissive and condescending—the pain in his leg was still intense, which couldn't have helped his mood.

Right away the questions began—where was Arnold getting his money?

❧

Arnold had been rich before the war, and he still had some money left. But there was more to it than that.

A few weeks before, while Arnold was still at Valley Forge, a merchant had come to see him in private. The merchant told Arnold that he had a ship in Philadelphia, the *Charming Nancy*, full of valuable merchandise. He wanted to get it out of town before the British army—or, for that matter, the American army—could get their hands on the goods. Arnold had written out a pass for the merchant, granting him permission to dock his ship at any American port, where, it was agreed, the goods would be sold to the highest bidder, and Arnold would get a share of the profits.

After he arrived in Philadelphia, Arnold learned that the *Charming Nancy* was docked in Egg Harbor, New Jersey, which was about to be attacked by the British. He quickly ordered twelve wagons to race to Egg Harbor "to remove property which was in imminent danger of falling into the hands of the enemy." These wagons belonged to the state of Pennsylvania and were supposed to be used only for government business—a detail to remember. The wagons returned loaded with linens, glass, sugar, tea, nails, and more. The goods were sold, and Arnold and his partner made a huge profit.

At the same time, while the city's shops were still closed, Arnold made secret agreements with merchants to buy up things the army wouldn't need. Soon the storerooms of the Penn mansion were stocked with expensive food and wine.

These private dealings may not have been technically illegal, though they were ethically questionable—Arnold knew enough to keep them secret. But there is no evidence he felt guilty about what he was doing. Quite the contrary, he seemed to think that civilians, who'd done nothing for the country, didn't deserve to get all the profits. The way Arnold saw it, he had sacrificed his health and most of his fortune for the cause of independence, and Congress had repeatedly failed to treat him with the respect he'd earned. So now he was just paying himself back—just taking what the country owed him.

Joseph Reed saw things very differently. The same age as Arnold, Reed was a successful lawyer, former aide to Washington, and current vice president of the Pennsylvania Executive Council, which ran the state. Like many politicians, Reed hated to see army leaders getting so popular, so influential. Reed was worried about the future of the republic—and possibly jealous of Arnold's fame. What was the point of overthrowing the British, he wondered, only to replace them with a homegrown nobility? Reed saw one solution: cut the military celebrities down to size, while there was still time.

From Reed's point of view, no one needed cutting down like Benedict Arnold. Passersby could almost see steam rising from Reed's head as he stood outside Arnold's headquarters, watching servants carry in crates of wine and wheels of cheese. He was sure Arnold was up to some shady business in there. And it made him crazy to see Arnold riding around in that gaudy coach, going to fancy balls, dinner parties, plays at John André's old theater—Reed particularly disapproved of plays, which he considered a frivolous distraction from the work of Revolution.

Arnold was not about to change to please Reed. At a ball in early July, he sat beside the dance floor, his foot propped on a pillowed stool. No longer able to dance, he enjoyed the music, watched the swirling figures, and flirted with the women who came over to his couch. He spotted a quiet young woman standing to the side, a pretty, shy-looking blonde. He asked an officer who she was.

The man told Arnold her name—Peggy Shippen.

Arnold asked to be introduced. She was led over and they chatted. He was smitten.

"I must tell you that Cupid has given our little general a more mortal wound than all the host of Britons could," a congressman's wife told a friend. "Miss Peggy Shippen is the fair one."

Peggy was intrigued as well, having heard so much about Arnold. "There can be no doubt," said one of Peggy's relatives, "the imagination of Miss Shippen was excited and her heart captivated by the oft-repeated stories of his gallant deeds, his feats of brilliant courage."

The day after the party, Arnold sent Peggy a lavish bouquet of flowers, throwing in a few nice bottles of wine for her father, Judge Shippen. Soon people began spotting Arnold's coach parked outside the Shippen mansion. They couldn't miss it—it was the fanciest one in town.

The best cobbler in the city made Arnold a special high-heeled shoe for his left foot, and with this shoe and a cane, he was finally able to walk without crutches. Arnold strolled the streets with a limp, tapping his gold-headed cane on the cobblestones, ignoring the raging storm around him.

The city was being torn apart by the same forces dividing the country. John Adams estimated that the American population was made up of about one-third Tories—

Loyalists, that is. Another third, he said, was "timid"—they just wanted the Revolution to go away. Only a third of the people were "true blue"—real Patriots.

In this charged atmosphere, even fashion took on political meaning. Prominent politicians like Joseph Reed took off their wigs, cut their hair short, and put on plain clothes—all as a way of symbolizing a complete break with Britain. Arnold liked the old ways. He kept right on wearing his tailored suits and, when he felt like it, his powdered wig.

Reed saw this as a sign that Arnold wasn't so "true blue" after all. And there were more signs. Arnold was known to invite women from politically suspect families to his dinner parties. "Will you not think it extraordinary," wrote Reed to General Nathaniel Greene, "that General Arnold made a public entertainment the night before last of which not only numerous Tory ladies, but the wives and daughters of persons proscribed by the state and now with the enemy in New York, formed a very considerable number?"

Again, this wasn't political to Arnold; he just enjoyed female company. "It is enough for me," he snapped back, "to contend with men in the field. I have not yet learned to carry on a warfare against women."

Everything was political, Reed insisted. "If things

proceed in the same train much longer," he warned, "I would advise every Continental officer to leave his uniform . . . and procure a scarlet coat as the only mode of ensuring respect."

Arnold sighed, saying of Reed, "There are many persons so unhappy in their dispositions, that, like the dog in the manger, they can neither enjoy the innocent pleasures of life themselves nor let others, without grumbling and growling, participate in them."

The result of all this public bickering was summed up by General Greene, who said, "Arnold has rendered himself not a little unpopular."

Arnold Under Attack

September 25, 1778–February 28, 1779

In September Arnold sat down to write Peggy Shippen a love letter. "Twenty times I have taken up my pen to write to you," he proclaimed, "and as often has my trembling hand refused to obey the dictates of my heart—a heart which, though calm and serene amidst the clashing of arms and all the din and horrors of war, trembles with diffidence and the fear of giving offense when it attempts to address you on a subject so important to its happiness."

These were almost the exact same lines he had written to Betsy DeBlois! Some historians believe that this proves that Arnold was insincere in his declaration to Peggy. But the same words can have different meanings in different settings, told to different people. Besides, Arnold was no poet. He was trying to force passion onto the page, doing the best he could.

"Do you feel no pity in your gentle bosom for the man who would die to make you happy?" he asked Peggy. "On you alone my happiness depends, and will you doom me to languish in despair?"

At the end he added a line on practical matters: "I have presumed to write to your Papa, and have requested his sanction to my addresses."

He sealed up the letter and sent it off.

Arnold's personal life was looking up, but his relationship with the Pennsylvania legislature was worsening by the day.

Soon after Arnold sent Peggy his love letter, Arnold's aide David Franks ran down the stairs of the Penn mansion in search of his barber. He called for a maid, who passed on Franks's wishes to William Matlack, a nineteen-year-old militiaman serving as a guard at Arnold's headquarters.

"Major Franks's orders were that I should fetch his barber," Matlack recalled. He grumbled, since he didn't think it was his duty, but went anyway. The barber wasn't in, so Matlack left a note asking him to come as soon as he could.

Back at his post at headquarters later that day, Matlack saw Franks coming down the stairs again, asking what had become of the barber. Matlack explained about the note. Franks waved his arms, emotionally declaring he did not believe the barber was really coming. He told Matlack to go again.

Matlack didn't go. "The militia cannot be expected to do such duty," he said, once Franks was gone.

Franks came down a third time. Astonished to see Matlack still standing there, he cried, "I thought I had ordered you to go for my barber!"

It was a stupid spat, but it turned serous that night when Matlack went home and complained to his father, Timothy, who happened to be one of James Reed's colleagues on the Pennsylvania Executive Council. Timothy Matlack wrote an angry note to Arnold. Arnold responded, agreeing that if Franks had insulted the boy, he should apologize. But, added Arnold, if Matlack didn't like taking orders, the military was not the place for him. "The respect due to a citizen," he explained, "is by no means to be paid to the soldier any further than his rank entitles him to it." To Arnold, that ended it.

But the Pennsylvania Council was just getting started. Members saw Franks's behavior as another example of military authorities acting like British aristocrats. Matlack wrote back, saying that if Arnold refused to punish Franks, he, Matlack, would be forced to pull his son from the militia and publish the reasons.

Arnold shot back, "If the declaration that you will withdraw your son from the service and publish the reason is intended as a threat, you have mistaken your object. I am not to be intimidated by a newspaper."

"Poor Peggy, how I pity her," said a relative of hers. "At any rate her situation must be extremely disagreeable."

Peggy's response to Arnold's love letter had been encouraging, but the public controversy was hardly helping Arnold's case with Judge Shippen. He had never liked Arnold and considered him a nobody who'd risen quickly to power and fame, and now, suddenly expected to be accepted among the leading families of Philadelphia. Besides, he seemed a bit wild.

Never one to back down, Arnold purchased Mount Pleasant, a mansion on ninety acres overlooking the Schuylkill River, one of the grandest estates in the city.

The judge was impressed. "They say she intends to surrender soon," Peggy's cousin said of her. "I thought the fort would not hold out so long. Well after all there is nothing like perseverance, and a regular attack."

❧

On December 1 James Reed became the president of the Pennsylvania Council, making him more powerful than ever. Still obsessed with taking Benedict Arnold down, Reed wondered where on earth Arnold got the money for a property like Mount Pleasant.

Reed and his allies began printing anonymous attacks in newspapers, hinting at corrupt dealings by "some gentleman of high rank, now in this city." Everyone knew exactly who the gentleman was.

Arnold should have ignored the articles, but as always, he just had to punch back. "This mode of attacking characters is really admirable," he wrote of the anonymous charges. "Equally as polite as conveying slander and defamation by significant nods, winks, and shrugs."

Then came another newspaper attack, this one much more brutal: "When I meet your carriage in the streets, and think of the splendor in which you live and revel . . . it is impossible to avoid the question, 'From whence have these riches flowed, if you did not plunder Montreal?'"

Arnold responded with open contempt toward Pennsylvania officials. When they questioned him about the use of the twelve wagons he'd sent to New Jersey, he refused to reply. "I shall only say," he told them, "that I am at all times ready to answer my public conduct to Congress or General Washington, to whom alone I am accountable."

Reed, deeply offended, complained to Congress of "the indignity offered us."

"Animosities run high between General Arnold and the executive branch of this State," noted a member of Congress. It was obvious to Arnold that he needed to get out of Philadelphia. In February 1779, he rode toward Washington's headquarters to talk over options. Reed panicked—alarmed at the idea of Arnold slipping away before Pennsylvania had a chance to make an example of him.

Arnold rode north through New Jersey on roads of mud and snow. He was near Washington's camp when his aide, Matthew Clarkson, galloped up and pulled a newspaper from his saddlebag.

Arnold took the paper and opened it—right to a list of formal charges brought by the Pennsylvania Executive Council against Benedict Arnold. The Council threw everything they could think of at Arnold: illegal purchases while the shops were closed, illegal use of public wagons for private gain, disrespectful treatment of militiaman, disrespect toward the leaders of Pennsylvania.

The charges were "abusive misrepresentations and calumnies," Arnold said, and his accusers "a set of wretches beneath the notice of a gentleman and a man of honor."

He continued on to Washington's camp, where he showed his commander the paper. The last thing Washington wanted was to step in the middle of this political brawl. He advised Arnold to go back to Philadelphia and deal with the problem.

Arnold walked out of Washington's cabin and stood in the mud. Washington could be cold, no question about it. In this case, he was just trying to avoid the appearance of favoring a general over civilian authorities. But to Arnold, it seemed as if Washington, too, now doubted him.

That night Arnold wrote another letter to Peggy. "Never did I so long to see or hear from you as at this instant," he began. "Six days' absence without hearing from my dear Peggy is intolerable."

He told her about his trip. "I am heartily tired with my journey and almost so with human nature," he wrote. "I daily discover so much baseness and ingratitude among mankind that I almost blush at being of the same species, and could quit the stage without regret were it not for some few gentle, generous souls like my dear Peggy."

The only thing that kept him going, he said, was the idea of getting back to her. "You alone, heard, felt, and seen, possess my every thought."

ANDRÉ IN NEW YORK

September 1778–April 1779

❧

John André spent the morning working at the big British army headquarters building in New York City. Then, early in the afternoon, he and the new British commander, General Henry Clinton, stepped outside, jumped onto horses, and rode north on Broadway.

They trotted through streets jammed with British soldiers, Loyalists who'd fled from other states, and escaped slaves. They rode past busy shops and taverns, crowded houses, burned-out buildings, and churches being used as hospitals. Soon they reached their favorite spot, a handball court between buildings. They hopped down from their horses, took off their jackets, and began to play.

This was a typical day for André now. As usual, he had landed on his feet in New York City, getting himself assigned to Clinton's staff, and quickly becoming

Clinton's closest aide. This was no easy task. Clinton was moody, distant, and a loner, the kind of guy who always seems annoyed with you, though you can never figure out why.

Other officers avoided Clinton, but André took a liking to him, somehow breaking through the man's icy crust. André was promoted to major. He began handling Clinton's mail and his schedule. Pretty soon other officers had to go through André just to get to the commander.

One morning André saw soldiers dragging two teenage boys through town. The soldiers tossed the boys in prison. Hearing one of the kids burst into tears, André decided to investigate.

They lived on a local farm, the boys explained. British soldiers had come through picking their family's crops— and they'd made the mistake of protesting.

"Well, well, my dear child," André said, "don't cry anymore."

André said he'd be right back. One of the boys asked the jailor who the man was.

"Why, that's Major André," said the jailor, "and you may thank your stars that he saw you, for I suppose that he has gone to the general to beg you off, as he has done for many of your damned rebel countrymen."

Sure enough, André returned soon, smiling. "Well, my boys, I've good news for you!" he announced. "The general has given you to me, to dispose of as I choose, and now you are at liberty. So run home to your fond parents, and be good boys."

André watched the boys run off. He was becoming an important man in New York—and loving it.

New York was nearly as much fun as Philadelphia—there was gambling, billiards, bowling, and all-night balls. André even helped open another theater and did a little writing and acting. But he was more serious now, more focused on his career. Knowing his close relationship with Clinton offered him a golden opportunity to advance, André worked night and day in Clinton's office.

Clinton rewarded the effort, making André his chief of intelligence in April 1779. André was just twenty-eight. Senior officers in New York found this extremely aggravating; one officer referred to André as "a cringing, insidious sycophant."

André was well aware that fellow officers resented his rapid rise. He was out on a ledge, and people were hoping to see him fall. There was only one way to solidify his shaky position—he would have to use his new intelligence position to pull off something big.

DELAY WORSE THAN DEATH
April 8–May 7, 1779

On the night of April 8, a small, curious crowd gathered outside the Shippen mansion in Philadelphia. Looking in through the lighted windows of the drawing room, they watched a brief wedding ceremony.

Peggy Shippen, in a gown, stood beside Benedict Arnold, who wore his blue and gold general's uniform. Unable to stand without a cane, Arnold leaned on the arm of his aide, Matthew Clarkson.

A bit later the newlyweds quietly stepped outside, climbed into Arnold's carriage, and drove off.

The charges against Arnold moved forward in the weeks after the wedding, and the now-famous case was front-page news all over the country. Benedict Arnold, said a fellow general, was now "served up as a constant dish of scandal to the breakfast of every table on the continent."

"I think the world are running mad," said Peggy's cousin Elizabeth Tilghman. "What demon has possessed the people with respect to General Arnold, he is certainly much abused; ungrateful monsters, to attack a character that has been looked up to, in more instances than one, since this war commenced."

Meanwhile, Arnold was running out of money. He put his New Haven house on the market, but there were no decent offers. He couldn't make the payments on Mount Pleasant, his new purchase, and had to rent it out to the Spanish ambassador. And all the while he was bleeding cash—clothes for himself and Peggy, living expenses for his sister Hannah, money for school for his three sons, all the entertaining he was expected to do in his official capacity as military governor, plus all the ongoing parties to celebrate the wedding.

Arnold's pay as a major general was $332 a month. When he got his pay, that is—Congress was often unable to come up with money to pay the army. And anyway, salaries were paid in Continental paper currency, which was worth less and less each day. As a point of reference, a nice pair of pants went for $1,000 in

Philadelphia shops that year. Arnold had to start bor-
rowing just to keep his household afloat.

For a while, at least, he was able to lock his troubles
outside. He and Peggy spent most of their time at home,
alone in their room. We'll never know exactly what they
talked about. But, based on later events, we can guess.

It was up to Congress to judge the case between Pennsylvania and Benedict Arnold. Most of the charges
seemed like trumped-up, politically motivated nonsense, which they were. As for the more serious charge
of illegal trading, Congress couldn't find any evidence—
Arnold had been guilty of shady dealings, but was much
too careful to leave a trail behind.

Members of Congress wanted to toss the whole
thing out, but were afraid of upsetting James Reed and
his powerful Pennsylvania Council. In the end, Congress dismissed a few of the sillier charges and passed
the others on to George Washington, telling him to try
Arnold in a military court.

Arnold wrote to Washington asking for a quick trial.
Reed objected, saying he needed more time to gather
evidence, threatening that if he didn't get his way the
state of Pennsylvania just might become a little less
supportive of Washington's war effort.

Washington was in an impossible position. "Dear Sir," he wrote to Arnold, "I find myself under a necessity of postponing your trial to a later period."

Arnold responded on May 5 with an incredible letter, one that gives us a bit of insight into his stormy state of mind. "If your Excellency thinks me a criminal," he wrote, "for heaven's sake let me be immediately tried and, if found guilty, executed."

Executed! No one was accusing Arnold of capital offenses; execution had nothing to do with the case.

"Having made every sacrifice of fortune and blood," he continued, "and become a cripple in the service of my country, I little expected to meet the ungrateful returns I have received from my countrymen; but as Congress have stamped ingratitude as a current coin, I must take it. I wish your Excellency, for your long and eminent services, may not be paid in the same coin. I have nothing left but the little reputation I have gained in the army. Delay in the present case is worse than death."

Why would a delay in the trial be worse than death? That's not entirely clear. Arnold was tormented by Reed and the mess he was in, but there's something more between those desperate lines. It's as though Arnold was wrestling with some demon, some dreadful decision. It almost sounds like he was begging Washington to save him before it was too late.

Just a few days later, Joseph Stansbury, a thirty-three-year-old amateur poet, closet Loyalist, and lover of fine clothes, was sitting in his glass and china shop in Black Horse Alley, by the Delaware River waterfront. Stansbury had known the Shippen family for years, and had sold them many fine pieces. So when one of Benedict Arnold's servants came into the shop, Stansbury figured the Arnolds must be in the market from some china.

He stopped by Arnold's headquarters that afternoon. Arnold showed Stansbury into his private office. Peggy was already there. They shut the door.

As it turned out, they didn't want any china.

Everything at Stake

May 10–May 30, 1779

❧

John André's new position as chief of intelligence had its drawbacks. People kept showing up in his office, saying they were spies, whispering crazy schemes, and requesting money for secret operations. André never knew which side these people were on, or what they really wanted.

It happened again on May 10. A man came into headquarters asking to see André. He was asked his business, but insisted he would speak only to André, and only privately.

The man was shown up to André's office. He introduced himself as Joseph Stansbury. André invited him in. The men made small talk for a while, chatting about Philadelphia and common acquaintances, including Peggy Shippen—now Peggy Arnold.

Then Stansbury dropped his bomb, telling André about his meeting with the Arnolds. "General Arnold," he said, "communicated to me, under a solemn obligation of secrecy, his intention of offering his services to the commander-in-chief of the British forces." Arnold had stated the goal, explained Stansbury, of helping to end the war, "either by immediately joining the British army or cooperating on some concealed plan with Sir Henry Clinton."

André sat silently, in shock. He and Clinton had made long lists of Americans they thought could be bought. They had never thought to write the name Benedict Arnold.

When he was able to speak, André told Stansbury to wait. He got up and walked to Clinton's office.

Five days later, Arnold sat in his Philadelphia office, suffering another excruciating attack of gout, unable to walk without help. An aide brought in a letter and handed it to Arnold. It was from George Washington—his response to Arnold's wild "delay is worse than death" note.

"I have received your favor of the 5th," wrote Washington, "and read it with no small concern. I feel my situation truly delicate and embarrassing." Washington assured Arnold that he too wished for a speedy trial, but for now they would both have to be patient. "I am sure you wish me to avoid even the semblance of partiality," he concluded. "I cautiously suspend my judgment till the result of a full and fair trial shall determine the merits of the prosecution."

It was typical Washington. And in any case, Arnold's decision had already been made. The message he really wanted came a bit later, when Joseph Stansbury returned with the response from André and Clinton. The news was good: they welcomed Arnold's offer of help.

Stansbury repeated André's reply word for word, "Should the abilities and zeal of that able and enterprising gentleman amount to the seizing of an obnoxious band of men, to the delivering into our power or enabling us to attack to advantage and by judicious assistance completely defeat a numerous body, then would the generosity of the nation exceed even his own most sanguine hopes."

André urged Arnold to propose something specific, a military plan of some sort. André explained one way they might communicate in the future. "The lady might write to me," he suggested. "The letters may talk of the *Meschianza* or other nonsense."

Of course "the lady" was Peggy Arnold. Between the lines of Peggy's innocent-sounding letter, Arnold could add his message in code, using invisible ink made from onion juice—the ink only became visible when exposed to heat.

Peggy and Benedict went to work on their coded reply. According to the system suggested by André, the code would be based on *Blackstone's Commentaries*, a massive legal text found in most well-read households. Each word of the coded message was made up of three numbers: a page number from *Blackstone's*, a line number, and a word number. So, for example, if Arnold wrote the sequence 124:25:7, André knew to turn to page 124, count down to the twenty-fifth line, and find the seventh word on that line. The writing and decoding process was slow and tedious, but it was a solid code—impossible to crack without knowing what book the correspondents were using.

"Sir Henry may depend on my exertions and intelligence," was Arnold's answer to André. "I will cooperate when an opportunity offers, and as life and everything is at stake, I shall expect some certainty—my property here secure and a revenue equivalent to the risk and service done."

Arnold asked for more details about money, saying, "inform me what I may expect." He ended with a p.s.: "Madame Arnold presents her particular complements"—his way of signaling that Peggy was in on any future plans.

André responded that Henry Clinton was eager to work with Arnold. "He can concur with you in almost any plan you can advise and in which you will cordially cooperate."

Arnold should use his knowledge and position to find a weak spot in the American army, André wrote. Then, together, they could strike the spot and win the war, and thus, said André, "put a speedy end to the miseries of our fellow creatures."

He offered Arnold some suggestions: "Join the army, accept a command, be surprised, be cut off. These things may happen in the course of a maneuver, nor you be censured or suspected. A complete service of this nature involving a corps of five or six thousand men would be rewarded with twice as many thousand guineas."

It was the first mention of a specific amount of money, which pleased Arnold. The message in André's note was clear. Arnold was extremely valuable to the British—but only if he could get back into an important command in the army.

❧

Arnold's court-martial was set to begin at Washington's New Jersey headquarters on June 1. Still not able to walk, he had to be lifted in and out of his carriage. When he arrived in camp he immediately cornered Washington and started cursing Congress and James Reed, pummeling his enemies with what Washington called "illiberal abuses." The commander coldly cut Arnold off, fearing that any conversation between them might open him to the charge of favoring Arnold in the coming trial.

"He self-invited some civilities I never meant to show him, or any officer in arrest," Washington said of the incident, "and he received rebuke."

If Arnold had been having any second thoughts, Washington's "rebuke" surely resolved them.

THE PRICE OF WEST POINT
June 1779–July 1780

❧

Just as Arnold's trial was getting underway, the war interfered. With the British army on the move, Washington postponed the trial and headed off with his army. Arnold was left behind with the sick and wounded. He waited three weeks. Then he went home.

Back in Philadelphia, Arnold continued his negotiations with André. Given what Arnold was risking, he wanted to make sure he was going to get paid, no matter what happened. Stansbury delivered this message to André, saying on behalf of Arnold, "He expects to have your promise that he shall be indemnified for any loss he may sustain in case of detection . . . that £10,000 shall be engaged to him for his services."

André's reply came in late July. He wanted to keep talking, but pointed out that for that kind of money—

equivalent to about $1.5 million today—Clinton would want something concrete, and very big. "Permit me to prescribe a little exertion," said André—in other words, he wanted Arnold to get back in action. "Would you assume a command and enable me to see you, I am convinced a conversation of a few minutes would satisfy you entirely, and I trust would give us equal cause to be pleased."

The negotiations were stuck. Arnold needed to make the next move by getting himself back into an important command in the army. But he couldn't do anything until his court-martial ended, and he had no idea when it might even start up again—it was delayed several more times through that summer and fall.

In October anger over rising food prices sparked riots in Philadelphia. Rioters tossed garbage, threw stones, and smashed windows, including those of Arnold's headquarters. When Arnold tried to restore order, he was chased and harassed, and only escaped by pulling out his pistol and threatening to fire.

"A mob of lawless ruffians have attacked me in the street and threatened my life," Arnold complained to Congress. He asked Congress to post guards outside his home. Congress passed the request on to the Pennsylvania Executive Council, which ignored it.

Benedict and Peggy locked their doors and stayed inside.

Arnold's court-martial finally resumed on December 23, in a tavern in Morristown, New Jersey. This was one of the strangest performances of Arnold's life, and that's saying a lot.

Limping loudly on the plank floor, he made his opening statement to the panel of generals and colonels. "It is disagreeable to be accused," he began. "When one is charged with practices which his soul abhors, and which conscious innocence tells him he had never committed, an honest indignation will draw from him expressions in his own favor.

"When the present necessary war against Great Britain commenced, I was in easy circumstances and enjoyed a fair prospect of improving them," continued Arnold. "I sacrificed domestic ease and happiness to the service of my country, and in her service have I sacrificed a great part of a handsome fortune."

For all he'd done, Arnold argued, he deserved better treatment. "The part which I have acted in the American cause has been acknowledged by our friends, and by our enemies, to have been far from an indifferent one.

My time, my fortune, and my person have been devoted to my country in this war."

He then presented the court with letters of thanks Washington and Congress had sent him over the years. "Is it probable," he asked the judges, "after having gained the favorable opinion of those whose favorable opinion it is an honor to gain, I should all at once sink into a course of conduct equally unworthy of the patriot and soldier?"

Arnold was trying to win a court case—he had to win to advance his plot with André. But those letters of praise still meant a lot to him. Even given what he was planning to do, he craved approval, especially from George Washington.

"Every method that men ingeniously wicked could invent has been practiced to blast and destroy my character," Arnold continued. "Such a vile prostitution of power and such instances of glaring tyranny and injustice I believe are unprecedented in the annals of any free people."

How could he be so self-righteous? After all, he *had* been guilty of devious dealings in Philadelphia. And he was at that moment plotting to betray his country! But therein lies the key to understanding Arnold: he didn't *feel* guilty. He was always able to convince himself that what he was doing was right. And if any feelings of remorse popped up, instead of dwelling on them he blended them with anger, and spewed them outward at his enemies.

Arnold went through the charges against him one at a time, refuting each in great detail. In conclusion, he returned to his main theme: "I have ever obeyed the calls of my country, and stepped forth in her defense in every hour of danger." He ended by apologizing for taking up so much of the court's time, saying he looked forward "with pleasing anxiety" to the court's decision. "I shall, I doubt not, stand honorably acquitted of all the charges brought against me."

On January 26, 1780, Arnold returned to the tavern to hear the court's decision. The panel acquitted him of all the serious charges, for which there was no evidence, ruling only that he had shown bad judgment. "The court," the judges concluded, "sentences him to receive a reprimand from his Excellency the commander-in-chief."

A slap on the wrist. Still, Arnold thought he deserved a full acquittal. "I ought to receive a reprimand," he complained. "For *what*?"

Washington, clearly wishing the whole thing would disappear, procrastinated two full months before following the court's directive. His reprimand was short and mild, referring, for instance, to Arnold's use of Pennsylvania's public wagons as "imprudent."

Washington followed that up with a personal letter for Arnold, one in which he practically apologized for the public reprimand. He urged Arnold to be more careful in the future. "Even the shadow of a fault tarnishes the luster of our finest achievements," he explained. But forget it, Washington said, and get back to work. "Exhibit anew those noble qualities which have placed you on the list of our most valued commanders. I will furnish you, as far as it may be in my power, with opportunities of regaining the esteem of your country."

It was a sensitive and generous note. But it came much too late.

On March 19 Peggy Arnold gave birth to a son, Edward. Two months later, unable to afford the Penn mansion anymore, the Arnolds moved into one of Peggy's father's houses. Biting back his pride, Arnold went to the French ambassador to ask for a loan. He was denied.

Sometime in May, Arnold started to think about

West Point. This American fort sat on a peninsula jutting into the Hudson River, about fifty miles north of New York City—such a strategically vital spot that Washington called West Point "the key to America." As long as the Americans held West Point, they could bottle British ships in New York City, preventing them from using the Hudson to slice into the countryside.

The more Arnold thought about West Point, the more interesting it looked. If he could get command there, he'd have an enormous bargaining chip. He pitched the idea to André, spelling out exactly what he expected as a reward: "If I point out a plan of cooperation by which S.H. [Sir Henry Clinton] shall possess himself of West Point, the garrison, etc., £20,000 I think will be a cheap purchase for an object of so much importance."

This got Clinton's attention. Now, finally, with the lure of West Point in the picture, André was able to get Clinton to commit to Arnold's price. "Should we through your means," André wrote to Arnold, "possess ourselves of three thousand men and [West Point's] artillery and stores with magazine of provisions for the army which may probably be there, the sum even of £20,000 should be paid you."

But André added a caution: Clinton was unwilling to

guarantee a large payment for effort alone. "As to an absolute promise of indemnification to the amount of £10,000," warned André, "whether services are performed or not, it can never be made."

Arnold could live with that. He'd just have to make sure he performed the services.

ATTACKING FORT ARNOLD
July 31–September 17, 1780

❧

George Washington sat on his horse on a hill above the Hudson River, watching soldiers cross the water on barges. He heard the beat of horse hooves, turned, and saw Benedict Arnold approaching. Washington was glad to see Arnold riding again, looking healthy, and ready for action.

But Arnold had been bugging the commander for weeks with a puzzling request—he wanted to be put in charge at West Point. Washington didn't like it. West Point was vital, yes, but it was strong enough already; the British were unlikely to attack. Why waste a two-fisted puncher like Arnold on a defensive assignment? Washington had a better idea.

Arnold rode up and stopped beside Washington on the riverbank, where the men exchanged friendly greetings.

Washington later said that Arnold "asked me if I had thought of anything for him."

Washington nodded, smiling with anticipation. Yes, he said, "a post of honor."

Arnold smiled, too, thinking he had West Point.

Washington then described the post: command of the left wing of Washington's army.

Arnold's smile collapsed, his cheeks clouded to a dark red.

"He appeared to be quite fallen," Washington said, "and instead of thanking me, or expressing any pleasure at the appointment, never opened his mouth."

Washington was visibly annoyed. He was offering Arnold one of the most important and prestigious jobs in the Continental Army, putting Arnold right back on top. Why didn't he leap at this, Washington wondered? Had all the trouble in Philadelphia broken his fighting spirit?

After a long, awkward silence, Washington asked Arnold to ride to headquarters and wait for him there. Arnold was soon seen limping back and forth in camp, complaining that his leg still wasn't right, that he couldn't ride properly, that only the West Point post would work for him.

Washington decided to try once more. He issued new orders on August 1, placing Arnold in command of his left wing. Peggy was at a dinner party when the news reached Philadelphia. Friends rushed in offering their congratulations.

When she asked why, they told her that her husband had just been placed in charge of Washington's left wing.

"This information affected her so much as to produce hysteric fits," said one friend. Peggy kept saying that there must be a mistake, that Arnold had actually been given the West Point command. "Efforts were made," said the friend, "to convince her that the general had been selected for a preferable station. These explanations, however, to the astonishment of all present, produced no effect."

Arnold went to Washington and again explained, really insisted, that he wasn't up to the physical demands of a command in the field. Reluctantly, on August 3, Washington issued revised orders: "Major General Arnold will take command of the garrison at West Point."

Washington was disappointed, but nothing more. "I had no more suspicion of Arnold than I had of myself," he later said.

British spies relayed the news to Clinton's headquarters in New York City. Now Clinton was starting to get excited. "General Arnold surrendering himself, the forts and garrisons, at this instant, would have given every advantage which could have been desired," he said.

The man he wanted in charge of this mission was John André. He promoted André to adjutant general of his army. The twenty-nine-year-old was now head of Clinton's staff—a post that usually went to much higher-ranking officers.

"Good fortune still follows me," André reported to his family in Britain. "I can hardly look back at the steep progress I have made without being giddy!" André was soaring too high, too fast, and he knew it. There was no way he could stay up there—not without pulling off something that would silence all of the critics.

Earlier in the war, the main fort at West Point had been named in Benedict Arnold's honor. So now Arnold had to figure out the best way to attack Fort Arnold.

He got right to work as soon he took command in early August, inspecting the grounds, taking notes. Right away people noticed something different about the general. "His head appeared to me bewildered from the very first moment he took command here," said a fellow officer.

Arnold's long-time aides, David Franks and Richard Varick, were worried, too. It particularly bothered them when Arnold started hanging around with a local dandy and wealthy landowner named Joshua Hett Smith. They had no idea that Smith had a leading role to play in Arnold's secret plan. Neither did Smith.

For his personal quarters, Arnold picked a Loyalist's abandoned mansion, just across the river from West Point. "It is surrounded on two sides by hideous mountains and dreary forests," said Dr. James Thacher, "not a house in view, and but one within a mile"—a perfect setting for the drama to come.

Now all Arnold needed was Peggy. He sent David Franks to Philadelphia to get her and the baby, writing out specific instructions on the route they should take, where they should stay each night, and more. "You must by all means get out of the carriage crossing all ferries or going over large bridges, to prevent accidents," he wrote. "You must not forget to bring your own sheets to sleep in on the road, and a feather bed to put in the light wagon, which will make an easy seat."

By this time Americans were getting sick of what was beginning to seem like an endless war. "Every idea you can form of our distresses will fall short of the reality," Washington told a friend. Dangerously underfed and hardly ever paid, soldiers were deserting the army—or erupting in violent mutinies. "There never has been a stage of the war in which the dissatisfaction has been so general and so alarming," Washington said.

Soldiers blamed Congress for the shortages; Congress resented the army's endless demands. States were squabbling amongst themselves, inflation was out of control, and growing numbers of civilians just wanted a return to peace.

Then Horatio Gates, hero of Saratoga, led an American army to a disastrous defeat at Camden, South Carolina. Actually, *led* is the wrong word—he panicked during the fighting, jumped on his horse, and turned up 180 miles from the battlefield. "An unfortunate piece of business to that hero," Arnold snickered.

By September 1780, the American Revolution was on the brink of collapse. "I have almost ceased to hope," said Washington.

∽

"The mass of the people are heartily tired of the war," Arnold wrote to André, "and wish to be on their former footing"—British citizens again, that is.

This was central to Arnold's plot. He was going to be well paid, but that was just the beginning. As a British general, he planned to lead Great Britain to a quick victory, thus ending the unpopular war and reuniting Britain and America in one peaceful and glorious empire. Arnold would be hailed as a hero in both lands, earn a colossal reward from King George—perhaps knighthood or a title of nobility.

It was audacious, insanely ambitious—and it was all falling into place. All that remained was for André and Arnold to meet in person to work out the final details. "It was certainly necessary that a meeting should be held with that officer for settling the whole plan," Clinton said.

André insisted on taking this mission himself. He knew it was risky, but, like Arnold, he knew the potential payoff. He and Arnold exchanged a final batch of coded letters. André would sail up the Hudson, anchor at an agreed-upon spot, wait until dark, then watch for a rowboat.

"I will send a person," said Arnold, "who will conduct you to a place of safety, where I will meet you."

On September 16 Arnold got an additional piece of news, one that raised the stakes even higher: George Washington and his staff were coming to West Point. Washington was on his way to Connecticut for talks with French generals and would be traveling without his army. He'd be in the West Point area for several days. He'd be easy prey.

"You will keep this to yourself," Washington told Arnold, "as I want to make my journey a secret."

Arnold passed the news on to André.

The Floating *Vulture*

September 19–September 22, 1780

On the afternoon of September 19, Clinton and his top officers gathered for a little party. Clinton was unusually talkative, almost giddy. He told everyone that André was leaving that night on a secret mission, one that might bring an end to the war. Before long, he said, they'd be referring to Major André as Sir John André.

"To Major André!" shouted an officer.

"Here, here!"

The others lifted their glasses and drank. They took turns leading songs. Soon it was André's turn. He hesitated. "I do feel rather serious this afternoon, and I can give no particular reason for it," he told the men. "I will sing, however, as you request me to." André chose an old army ballad, and his voice seemed to tremble as he began:

Why, soldiers why
Should we be melancholy, boys?
Why, soldiers why,
Whose business is to die . . .

After the meal, Clinton took André aside. Knowing his young officer lacked experience in intelligence missions, Clinton emphasized three essential points. One: do not go behind American lines. Two: refuse to carry incriminating papers. Three: no matter what, do not take off your British uniform. If anything goes wrong, Clinton explained, these rules will protect you from the charge of spying—and certain execution.

André agreed. That night he sailed north on the Hudson aboard a ship named *Vulture*.

Arnold saw the *Vulture* reach the agreed-upon spot. He had to get André, and he had to do it without involving any American soldiers—it would look too suspicious for him to be meeting with someone from the British ship.

Arnold waited for dark, then turned to his carefully chosen tool, the unsuspecting Joshua Hett Smith. Arnold told Smith that there was a man named John Anderson aboard the *Vulture*, a merchant, with intelligence that could help the Americans. Arnold explained that he needed Smith to row out to the British ship, pick Anderson up, and bring him to shore. It was secret business, Arnold added, he could say nothing more.

Smith was thrilled to be involved in something so exciting. He went to the home of one of his tenant farmers, Samuel Cahoon.

"Mr. Smith spoke to me as I was going for the cows," Cahoon recalled. "I went up with Mr. Smith in the room where General Arnold was."

Arnold explained that Cahoon and his brother were going to row Smith's small boat out to the *Vulture*.

"I said I could not go," Cahoon said, "and told him I was afraid to go, but General Arnold urged me to go, and told me if I was a friend to my country I should do my best."

Cahoon went home to get his brother.

"I was sorry I was wanted for that purpose," remembered the brother, Joseph, "and said upon any other thing I was willing to serve."

Then Samuel's wife heard where the brothers were going. She told them not to go.

"My wife being dissatisfied with my going," Samuel Cahoon said, "I went back to General Arnold, and told him that I did not want to go."

"It must be done for the good of the country," insisted Arnold.

When that didn't do it, Smith began pouring the brothers big cups of rum. Arnold promised them a reward of fifty pounds of flour each. They never got that flour.

Finally, a little after midnight, Smith and the tipsy Cahoons walked down to the waterside where Smith's rowboat was tied up. They wrapped sheepskins around the oars to muffle their sound, pushed out into Hudson, and rowed silently toward the *Vulture*.

"The night was serene, the tide favorable," Smith said. "Although the distance was nearly twelve miles, we soon reached the ship."

Sailors on the ship—who had no idea what Arnold and André were up to—angrily called for the midnight visitors to identify themselves.

"Friends!" shouted Smith.

The sailors were unconvinced. "I was heartily assailed with a volley of oaths, all in the peculiarity of sea language," recalled Smith.

The Cahoons eased their boat alongside the British ship.

"Hoist the Rebel rascal on board!" one sailor shouted.

Smith was yanked onto the deck. The curses and threats continued until a cabin boy came up and said, "The captain orders the man below."

André had been lying in bed in his uniform, wondering what was taking so long. When he heard the shouting on deck he stood up. He took a long blue coat from a nail on the wall, put it on over his red uniform jacket, buttoned it up, and left his cabin.

A few minutes later, he and Smith climbed down into the rowboat. Smith steered while the Cahoon brothers rowed back toward shore. It was a dark, moonless night.

"Very little conversation passed between Mr. Anderson and myself," Smith said, "excepting trivial remarks about the tide, the weather, and matters of no concern. Mr. Anderson, from his youthful appearance and the softness of his manners, did not seem to me to be qualified for a business of such moment."

Arnold stood on the bank above the river, hidden by fir trees, waiting and listening. He knew he'd hear the boat before he saw it, and there it was—the grind of wood on sand, the splash of a boot hitting water.

Smith climbed up the bank and told Arnold that

Anderson was here. John André walked up and stood in the tiny clearing.

Arnold told Smith to go back down to the boat. "I went as directed," grumbled Smith, "but I felt greatly mortified at not being present at the interview, to which I conceived myself entitled from my rank in life and the trouble I had taken to effect the meeting."

Arnold and André stood in that dark spot between the trees, talking in whispers until 4:00 a.m.

Smith sat by the river, shivering, listening to the snoring Cahoon brothers. When he saw the sky beginning to lighten above the mountains to the east, he climbed back up the bank and interrupted Arnold and André to tell them that dawn was coming.

Arnold told Smith to take Mr. Anderson back to the *Vulture*. Smith and André walked down to the boat and woke the Cahoons, who refused to make another trip. André pleaded with them.

"I told him I was fatigued," Samuel Cahoon said, "and could not go."

As the men argued in whispers they realized it was too late anyway—the sun was already rising. "I was told that the approach of day would prevent my return," André said, "and that I must be concealed until the next night."

Arnold and André got onto horses. As Arnold led the way up through the woods, American guards stepped out, recognized Arnold, and saluted him.

André had thought he was on neutral ground, between British and American-held territory. But those soldiers standing guard proved otherwise. He was behind American lines. He'd just violated the first of Clinton's three orders.

Arnold led André back to Smith's house, where the two men went to an upstairs bedroom and shut the door. André took off his overcoat.

Smith arrived, prepared some breakfast, and brought it upstairs. He was stunned to see his guest wearing a red British uniform jacket—Arnold had told him that André was a merchant.

The men sat down to eat. "He seemed shy, and desirous to avoid much conversation," Smith said of André. "He continued to urge preparations for his departure, and carefully avoided being seen by persons that came to the house."

The meal was interrupted by the sound of explosions coming from the river below. All three men rushed to the window.

∽

That morning at sunrise, an American officer named James Livingston had been surprised to see the *Vulture* floating in the river south of West Point. Annoyed to see a British ship so close to American lines, he had pulled two tiny cannon down to the river. No one ordered him to do this—it just seemed like a good idea.

"Firing at a ship with a four-pounder, is in my opinion, a waste of powder," Colonel John Lamb told Livingston.

Livingston decided to try it anyway. It was the sound of his booming guns that sent André, Arnold, and Smith racing to the window of Smith's house.

For two hours Livingston and his crew blasted their guns at the *Vulture*. Six of their shots crashed through the ship's hull.

"Many others struck the sails, rigging, and boats on deck," said a British officer aboard the *Vulture*. "Captain Sutherland is the only person hurt, and he very slightly on the nose by a splinter."

But it was a splinter that changed the course of history. The captain ordered the *Vulture* to drop back out of range of American guns.

André watched it all from the window of Smith's

house. The British ship—the ship that was supposed to take him back to safety in New York City—drifted south with the current and was soon out of view.

"He cast an anxious look toward the *Vulture*," Smith said, "and with a heavy sigh, wished he was on board."

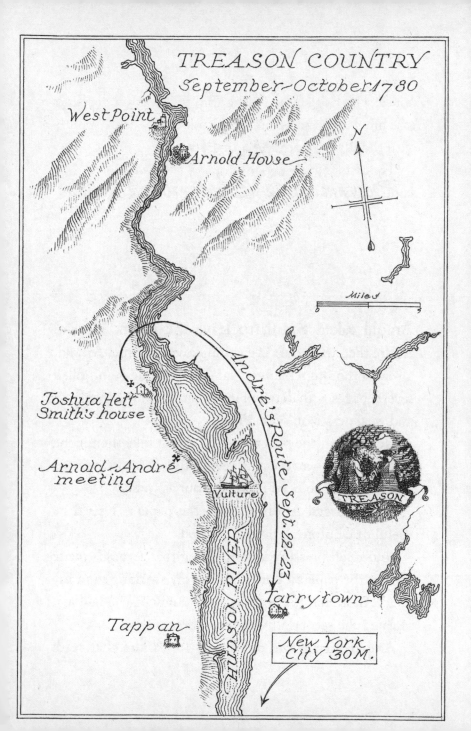

TREASON COUNTRY
September–October 1780

West Point

Arnold House

N

Miles

André's Route Sept. 22–23

Joshua Hett
Smith's house

Arnold–André
meeting

Vulture

TREASON

HUDSON RIVER

Tarrytown

Tappan

New York
City 30 M.

NO-MAN'S LAND

September 22–September 23, 1780

Arnold asked Smith to leave the room. He and André then went over everything one last time. Arnold, always a thorough planner, sat down at a desk and filled several pages with detailed information on the strengths and weaknesses of West Point.

He held out the papers. André didn't take them. The men had gone over the plan several times, André pointed out. Why did he need it written out as well?

Arnold urged André to take the papers. They'd be useful to Clinton, Arnold explained.

André felt pressured, later saying that Arnold "made me put the papers I bore between my stockings and my feet." André put his boot back on, knowing he had just violated the second of Clinton's three orders.

Arnold then wrote out a pass for André that read:

"Permit Mr. John Anderson to pass the guards . . . he being on public business in my direction. B. Arnold, Maj. General."

That would get André past any American soldiers he might meet. It was agreed that as soon as André made it back to New York City and shared his intelligence with Clinton, the British attack would begin. If it was timed just right, they would get the fort, thousands of soldiers, George Washington—everything.

André couldn't set out until dark. He lay down to take a nap.

Smith was outside, meanwhile, having the time of his life. When people he knew passed the house he pulled them aside and said, listen, I can't talk right now, I'm on an important mission for General Arnold and his secret agent.

Arnold came down and found Smith. They looked toward the river. The *Vulture* was too far away to reach by rowboat, Arnold explained. Their guest would have to ride back to British lines. Smith would ride with him and show him the way.

Smith agreed, but wanted to know why the man was wearing a British uniform.

Oh, that, said Arnold, that's nothing. He borrowed

it from a British officer and just wears it out of vanity. Of course, Arnold pointed out, he'll have to take it off before riding across American territory back toward New York City.

Smith said he'd loan André some new clothes. Arnold climbed onto his horse and rode back home to update Peggy. There had been a few minor glitches. Otherwise, it was all working out.

Late that afternoon André stood in the bedroom of Smith's house, wearing borrowed clothes: a beaver hat and a frayed and faded purple jacket with gold-laced buttons. "I was induced to put on this wretched coat," André said later. It wasn't just bad fashion—André had violated Clinton's third and last order.

"At the decline of the sun, I set out on horseback," André said. He rode along with Smith and a third rider, Smith's young African American slave. No one worried about what the slave heard or saw—slaves couldn't testify in court. Smith chatted endlessly as they rode. He had no idea why Anderson was so quiet and nervous.

The road was winding and hilly, passing through dark forests and occasional clearings with farms. At about nine o'clock a voice came from the roadside darkness: "Who goes there?"

"Friends," said Smith. He glanced at André. "Mr. Anderson seemed very uneasy," Smith recalled.

Soldiers stepped into the road, pointing muskets at the riders.

Smith turned to the captain in charge. "I told him who I was, and that we had passports from General Arnold," Smith said, "that we were on the public service, on business of the highest import, and that he would be answerable for our detention one moment."

The captain asked to see Arnold's pass. Smith handed it over. The captain motioned for a lantern to be brought closer, and he inspected the paper in the faint light. It looked okay.

He handed back the pass, but warned Smith to go no farther that night. Smith knew why. The next fifteen miles or so were a violent no-man's land, controlled neither by the Americans nor the British. Roving gangs known as Cowboys—Loyalist-leaning thugs—fought for territory and loot with gangs known as Skinners—Rebel-leaning thugs. "No one slept safely in his bed," Smith said of this territory. "Many families hid themselves at night in barns, wheat-ricks, corn-cribs, and stacks of hay."

Smith hesitated, unsure what to do. "My companion," he said of André, "expressed his wish to proceed; but the captain suggested many prudential reasons why he would not advise our progress at night."

Smith led André to a nearby farmhouse and knocked. There was no answer. He had to bang for several minutes before a frightened farmer opened the door a crack. The man looked Smith and André over, let them in, showed them to a tiny bedroom, and locked them inside.

"We slept in the same bed," Smith said, "I was often disturbed with the restless motions and uneasiness of mind exhibited by my bed-fellow."

André never even took off his boots. "He appeared in the morning," said Smith, "as if he had not slept an hour during the night. He at first was much dejected."

It was cool and foggy when they got back on the road. André saw an American coming toward them and recognized the man as Colonel Webb, who'd been a prisoner in New York City when André was there; he knew André's face. André and Webb rode toward each other on the narrow path. Webb seemed to be staring at André, and André felt the hair standing up under his ridiculous borrowed hat.

Webb rode right past.

The rising sun burned off the fog, and the morning

turned warm. André's mood improved steadily as the men rode farther south.

"I now found him highly entertaining," said Smith. "He was not only well informed in general history, but well acquainted with that of America . . . he conversed freely on the belles letters: music, painting, and poetry."

They stopped at a farmhouse for some quick breakfast. The woman there told them everything had been stolen, except one cow and some cornmeal. She made a quick porridge of corn and milk, and the riders sat on her back step, scooping it up. "We made a good meal," said Smith, "our appetites being keen from having been supperless the preceding night."

When they finished eating, Smith stunned André by saying that he was too frightened to ride any farther south. He gave André directions, describing the roads he'd need to take back to British lines. Then he and his slave rode off.

André continued alone. All along the road were signs of the ongoing war between Cowboys and Skinners: abandoned houses, overgrown fields, wasps feasting on rotting piles of fruit beneath the trees. At a few homes André saw eyes peeking out from parted curtains.

He stopped at a farmhouse and rode to the well. Surprised to see two children watching him, he asked if he could have a drink. The girl, about twelve, filled a cup and handed it up to André. The boy, a bit older, held the reigns of André's horse while he drank. André handed down a coin, thanked them, and rode on.

A few miles ahead, in the town of Tarrytown, three men crouched in the trees beside the road—John Paulding, David Williams, and Isaac Van Wart. Were they American militiamen, or pro-American Skinners looking to rob Loyalists? That's not clear—a bit of both, most likely.

They were hidden beside a small bridge, just a few logs laid over a stream. At about nine thirty in the morning they heard the pounding of hooves approaching the bridge.

Williams took a look and said to the others, "Here comes a gentleman-like man, who appears well dressed, and whom you had better step out and stop, if you don't know him."

No one knew the rider. The men stepped into the road.

PAPERS OF A DANGEROUS TENDENCY
September 23–September 25, 1780

❧

André relaxed a bit as he passed through Tarrytown. As he crossed a small bridge, he could see British territory in the distance.

Suddenly, he nearly crashed into three men blocking the road. One of the men grabbed the bit of André's horse, yanking it to a stop. The others pointed guns at André. He had a split second to decide how to play this.

Thinking he was safely past Skinner country, André said, "My lads, I hope you belong to our party."

"What party?" demanded Paulding.

"The lower party," said André, meaning lower as in farther south—the British. "Thank God, I am once more among friends, I am glad to see you. I am an officer in the British service, and have now been on particular business in the country, and I hope you will not detain me."

The men stared up at André, but said nothing.

André pulled out his gold watch, saying, "And for a token to let you know I am a gentleman—"

Paulding cut him short, "Get down. We're Americans."

André's face went paper white. "God bless my soul," he finally managed, attempting a laugh, "a body must do anything to get along nowadays."

André pulled out Arnold's pass. Paulding, the only one of the three who could read, grabbed it and studied it.

"Had he pulled out General Arnold's pass first, I should have let him go," Paulding later said. But now he was suspicious. "Damn Arnold's pass!" he said. "You said you was a British officer. Get down. Where's your money?"

"Gentlemen, you had best let me go," André said, "or you will bring yourselves in trouble, for, by stopping me, you will detain the general's business."

"God damn it!" shouted Paulding. "Where is your money?"

"Gentlemen, I have none about me."

"You are a British officer, and no money? Let's search him!"

The men pushed André into the woods beside the

road and ordered him to strip. Starting with Smith's purple coat, André took off each piece of clothing. He stood in the dirt, completely naked but for boots and stockings, watching his captors rip his clothes apart in search of loot. Between his foot and stocking he could feel Arnold's folded papers.

"Damn him!" shouted one of them. "He may have it in his boots!"

They yanked off André's boots and reached inside. Nothing. They were about to give up and let the man get dressed, when Van Wart noticed something. "We found his stockings sagged a little," he said.

With a gun barrel at his chest, André lifted his feet and pulled off his stockings. The men turned them inside out. The papers fell to the ground. Paulding snatched them up and began to read, puzzling over the words, the meaning.

He looked up, shouting, "This is a spy!"

André denied it, demanding to be set free.

They asked him what freedom was worth to him.

"Any sum you want," André replied.

"A hundred guineas," asked Williams, "with the horse, saddle, bridle, and your watch?"

"Yes, and the money shall be sent here if you want."

"Will you not give more?"

"Yes."

They went back and forth until André offered the outrageous sum of ten thousand golden guineas.

The men were torn. It was a tempting reward, but collecting from the British would be risky. It was safer to turn him in to the Americans, and it might be worth something—the man was certainly acting like he was worth something.

"You could read in his face that he thought it was all over with him," Van Wart said.

André dressed quickly. As he was led away he told his captors, "I would to God you had blown my brains out when you stopped me."

Joshua Hett Smith rode back to Arnold's house, proud of a job well done. He strolled in just as the Arnolds, along with a few staff members and West Point officers, were sitting down to a meal.

Smith bent toward Arnold's ear and whispered the news: John Anderson was safely on his way to New York City.

Arnold nodded and invited Smith to have a seat. Arnold's aides, Franks and Varick, looked at each other, irritated that this clown should be welcome at Arnold's table.

It was a quiet meal. Colonel John Lamb remembered that Peggy broke the silence by asking for more butter. "She was informed by the servant that there was no more," he said.

"Bless me," said Arnold, "I forgot the olive oil I bought in Philadelphia. It will do very well with salt fish."

The servant brought the oil. It was quality stuff, Arnold commented as he poured, and had cost him eighty dollars.

Smith chuckled loudly. "You mean eighty cents," he said, mocking the nearly worthless American currency.

Glaring at Smith, Varick nearly screamed, "That is not true, Mr. Smith!"

The table exploded. Varick and Franks yelled at Smith, Arnold yelled at Varick and Franks, Peggy yelled for everyone to shut up.

The rest of the meal was eaten in tense silence, broken only by the sounds of the chewing of salt fish.

Aboard the *Vulture*, the crew was getting nervous. Where was André? That night an officer on the ship sent Clinton a distressing update: "It is with the greatest concern that I must now acquaint your Excellency that we have not heard the least account of him since he left the ship."

André spent the night at an American army post, where he was delivered by his three captors. The post commander, Colonel John Jameson, was unsure what to do with the prisoner. The man's pass from Arnold was genuine. But why would he be heading into British territory with plans of West Point in his sock?

On the one hand, Jameson was not prepared to openly accuse Arnold of plotting with the prisoner. On the other hand, he couldn't just let this so-called John Anderson go, no matter what his pass said. He compromised. He sent notice to Arnold that the prisoner had been taken with incriminating papers. At the same time, he sent the papers themselves on to George Washington.

The messengers rode through the night, one toward Arnold, the other toward Washington.

Washington and his staff were camped very close. The messenger with Washington's package galloped past the general, was told he'd gone too far, and turned around.

Meanwhile, Washington decided to take an early morning ride. He and his staff rode along the Hudson, studying the land and forts surrounding West Point. They were expected at Arnold's house for breakfast, but

Washington was in no hurry—he kept stopping, looking around, inspecting the ground, and making mental notes.

General Lafayette was getting anxious. "General, you are going in a wrong direction," he said to the commander, "you know Mrs. Arnold is waiting breakfast for us."

Washington smiled at the young French volunteer. "Ah, I know you young men are all in love with Mrs. Arnold, and wish to get where she is as soon as possible," he teased. "You may go and take your breakfast with her, and tell her not to wait for me."

Embarrassed, Lafayette said he could wait. But it was decided to send two officers ahead to tell Arnold that Washington and the staff would be a little late.

By the time the two officers reached Arnold's house, Arnold was already sitting at the breakfast table. He invited the men to join him.

Just as the coffee was being poured, a muddy messenger ran in and handed Arnold a note. It was from Colonel Jameson.

Arnold unfolded the paper and scanned the writing and his eyes caught the phrase, "a certain John Anderson taken going into New York."

One of the two officers sent by Washington, Major

James McHenry, was watching Arnold. "I observed in him an embarrassment and agitation so unusual that I knew not to what to attribute it," he said.

Arnold read on. "He had a passport signed in your name. He had a parcel of papers taken from under his stockings, which I think of a very dangerous tendency. The papers I have sent to General Washington."

Washington would be there any minute. Had he already gotten the papers? Arnold had no way of knowing. He excused himself and stood up.

Arnold limped and leaped up the stairs to Peggy's bedroom and slammed the door behind him. She was still in bed.

Arnold blurted out the news. He would have to leave immediately.

There was a knock on the door. Arnold froze.

"His Excellency is nigh at hand," said Franks through the door.

Peggy fainted.

Arnold charged out of the room "in great confusion," Franks said. "And, ordering a horse to be saddled, mounted him, and told me to inform his Excellency that he was gone over to West Point and would return in about an hour."

Arnold galloped toward the river. Blocking the road in front of him stood four members of George Washington's personal guard. Arnold reached for his pistol. The men saluted him, stepped out of his way.

Arnold jumped off his horse at the edge of the river, where his small boat was tied up. Several soldiers were standing around—it was their job to be there for Arnold whenever he needed to be rowed somewhere. He hopped into the boat and ordered the men to get on and push off immediately. As they rowed away from shore, Arnold told the men to hurry south, toward the *Vulture*, saying he had secret business with a man on board the British ship.

Arnold took out his pistols, checked the powder, and cocked them. He stood with his guns in his hands.

A SCENE TOO SHOCKING
September 25, 1780

Just minutes after Arnold left his headquarters, Washington arrived. He was told Arnold had just left for West Point. Washington and his staff had a quick breakfast, then rowed across the river to the fort.

Always a stickler for official procedure, Washington was expecting a formal greeting at West Point, complete with the appropriate thirteen-cannon salute. There was nothing. The boat reached shore and Washington and his men got out. No one was there to meet him.

Up in the fort, Colonel Lamb finally noticed the commander-in-chief standing on the muddy riverbank, looking annoyed. Lamb raced down.

"Is not General Arnold here?" demanded Washington.

"No, sir," said Lamb. "We have not seen him on this side of the river today."

"The impropriety of his conduct when he knew I was to be there struck me very forcibly," Washington later said. "But I had not the least idea of the real cause."

Then, as he inspected West Point, he began to see that something was very wrong. The fort looked neglected. Guns and soldiers were out of position. The place was wide open to attack.

Back at Arnold's house, Richard Varick was lying on a downstairs couch, getting a little rest.

"I heard a shriek," he said. He jumped up and ran up the stairs to Peggy's room. "And there met the miserable lady, raving, distracted," he remembered, "with her hair disheveled and flowing about her neck."

She was sitting up in bed, wearing only a thin nightgown, nearly transparent in the bright sunlight streaming through the windows.

"She seized me by the hand," Varick said, "with this—to me—distressing address and a wild look."

"Colonel Varick," cried Peggy, "have you ordered my child to be killed?"

Varick was stunned. Peggy jumped out of the bed and fell at his knees, begging him to spare her baby. "A scene too shocking for my feelings," Varick said. "I attempted to rise her up, but in vain."

ST E V E   S H E I N K I N

She continued crying, saying she'd been left all alone.

"I told her she had Franks and me," Varick said, "and General Arnold would soon be home from West Point with General Washington."

"No, General Arnold will never return!" screamed Peggy. "He is gone, he is gone forever!" Pointing to the ceiling she added, "There, there, there, the spirits have carried him up there, they have put hot irons on his head!"

"This alarmed me much," said Varick.

Washington and his staff soon returned from West Point, expecting to find Arnold at home. No one knew where he'd gone.

Not until a messenger ran in. This was the man sent by Colonel Jameson—he'd been chasing Washington, just missing him, all day. Now he finally handed Washington the packet of papers taken from John André's stocking.

Washington took the papers. He immediately recognized Arnold's handwriting. The other officers watched Washington read. They thought they saw his hands shaking.

Washington looked up. "Arnold has betrayed me," he said. "Whom can we trust now?"

"A search was made for Arnold," said Lafayette, "but he had escaped in a boat."

With Arnold out of reach, Washington turned his attention to preparing West Point for a British attack. "I request you will be as vigilant as possible," he told the fort's officers. "The enemy may have it in contemplation to attempt some enterprise, even tonight."

He called in his best soldiers from New Jersey, Connecticut, and Massachusetts, and put one of his top generals, Nathaniel Greene, in charge at West Point. There was no time to explain why, Washington wrote to Greene, "Transactions of a most interesting nature, and such as will astonish you, have been just discovered."

When she heard Washington's voice downstairs, Peggy asked to see the commander. Varick brought him up.

As Washington stepped into the room, Peggy began raving again, insisting this was not General Washington.

"The general assured her he was," Varick recalled.

"No, that is not General Washington!" she shrieked. "That is the man who is going to assist Colonel Varick in killing my child!"

Washington sat stiffly on the edge of the bed, trying to comfort Peggy. This sort of thing was not Washington's strong suit.

"It was the most affecting scene I ever was witness to," said one of Washington's young aides, Alexander Hamilton. "She for a considerable time entirely lost her senses . . . one moment she raved, another she melted into tears. . . . All the sweetness of beauty, all the loveliness of innocence, all the tenderness of a wife and all the fondness of a mother showed themselves in her appearance and conduct."

Had Peggy Arnold really "lost her senses"? Or was it the acting job of the century, made more believable by the real terror she was feeling? No one knows for sure. What's clear is that it was very much in Peggy's interest to convince Washington that she had no part in her husband's treachery. She did that.

"The unhappy Mrs. Arnold did not know a word of this conspiracy," Lafayette told a friend. "General Washington and everyone else here sympathize warmly with this estimable woman, whose face and whose youthfulness make her so interesting."

Soon after Washington left the room, Peggy calmed down, and lay quietly in bed.

It was less quiet at the home of Joshua Hett Smith.

"The door of the room wherein I lay in bed with Mrs. Smith was forced open with great violence," remembered Smith. "And instantly the chamber was filled with soldiers, who approached the bed with fixed bayonets. I was then, without ceremony, drawn out of bed."

The soldiers dragged Smith to Arnold's house and tossed him into a room with Washington.

"I addressed General Washington, and demanded to know for what cause I was brought before him," said Smith. "The general answered sternly, that I stood before him charged with the blackest treason against the citizens of the United States."

Smith was confused. Treason? He had been following the orders of General Arnold.

Washington erupted. "Sir, do you know that Arnold has fled, and that Mr. Anderson, whom you have piloted through our lines, proves to be Major John André, the Adjutant-General of the British army, now our prisoner?"

Smith insisted he hadn't known.

Washington pointed toward the window and shouted, "Unless you confess who were your accomplices, I shall suspend you from that tree!"

Smith again protested his innocence.

Washington took a few deep breaths and began to calm down. The more Smith talked, the more likely it seemed that he was a patsy, that he really knew nothing. Washington had Smith thrown in jail, just in case.

Washington and his staff stayed up all night, waiting for a British attack that never came. At some point they tried to eat something.

"Never was there a more melancholy dinner," remembered Lafayette. "The General was silent and reserved, and none of us spoke of what we were thinking about."

The men picked at their food, avoiding eye contact. "Gloom and distrust seemed to pervade every mind," Lafayette said. "I have never seen General Washington so affected by any circumstance."

READY AT ANY MOMENT
September 26–October 2, 1780

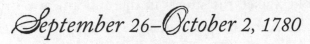

"I have ever acted from a principle of love to my country."

So wrote Benedict Arnold, from the deck of the *Vulture*, to George Washington. True to character, Arnold had already convinced himself he'd been in the right, even acted nobly. "The same principle of love to my country actuates my present conduct," he wrote, "however it may appear inconsistent to the world, who very seldom judge right any man's actions."

Guess how well that went over with Washington.

Arnold did do one decent thing. "In justice to the gentlemen of my family," he wrote, "Colonel Varick and Major Franks, I think myself in honor bound to declare that they, as well as Joshua Smith, who I know is suspected, are totally ignorant of any transactions of mine that they had reason to believe were injurious to the public."

The *Vulture* sailed back to New York City, where Arnold walked the streets in the uniform of a British general. A few people nodded to him. Most just stared icily. It was not the reception he had hoped for.

Arnold's arrival had stunned the city—a ship about to sail for Britain was actually held in port while people in town wrote letters home with the news. But when the shock of seeing Arnold wore off, all anyone wanted to talk about was John André. Where was André? What was going to happen to him?

Henry Clinton was a wreck. "The general has escaped to us," he wrote, "but we have lost—how shall I tell it to you—poor André. I am distressed beyond words." The rest of the officers took their cue from Clinton; if Clinton wasn't going to welcome Arnold, neither were they.

Arnold walked the streets in his new uniform, more alone than he'd ever been. His plot was a failure. If André died, the catastrophe would be complete.

André rode along the Hudson River, surrounded by a small army of American soldiers. He had confessed his true identity, and was being taken to George Washington, who would decide his fate.

Beside André rode a young American officer named Benjamin Tallmadge. The men chatted as they traveled. As casually as he could, André brought up the question: What do you think they'll do to me?

Tallmadge asked André if he'd ever heard of Nathan Hale, who'd been caught spying on the British in New York City several years earlier. "Do you recall his fate?"

"Yes," said André, "he was hanged as a spy, but surely you do not consider his case and mine alike!"

"They are precisely similar," said Tallmadge, "and similar will be your fate."

Until that moment André had thought the Americans considered him a prisoner of war. This was much more serious.

He was locked in a small stone house in the town of Tappan, near Washington's headquarters. His room had a small window looking out at a church. Two guards stayed with him at all times.

Washington arranged a quick trial. He excused himself, but placed all his generals on the panel of judges. One of André's judges was Henry Knox—the jolly officer who'd spent a pleasant night chatting with André in a roadside inn nearly five years before.

André's trial was brief and simple. He had been caught

behind enemy lines, disguised as a civilian, with Arnold's papers hidden on him. According to the rules of war, André was a spy.

"It is not possible to save him," said General Steuben. "He put to us no proof, but in an open, manly manner, confessed everything."

"He behaved with so much frankness, courage, and delicacy," said Lafayette, "that I could not help lamenting his unhappy fate."

Like most people who met André, the judges were charmed and impressed. But the decision was unanimous: "Major André, Adjutant General of the British Army, ought to be considered a spy from the enemy, and that, agreeable to the law and usage of nations, it is their opinion he ought to suffer death."

Alexander Hamilton sat with André in his prison that night.

"I foresee my fate, and, though I pretend not to play the hero, or to be indifferent about life, yet I am reconciled to whatever may happen," André told Hamilton. "There is only one thing that disturbs my tranquility. Sir Henry Clinton has been too good to me . . . I would not for the world leave a sting in his mind that should embitter his future days."

"He could scarce finished the sentence," Hamilton said, "bursting into tears."

In New York City, Clinton kept calling meetings of generals to discuss options, ways to save André. He couldn't make it through them without weeping.

He received a note from the prisoner. "I have obtained General Washington's permission to send you this letter," wrote André, "the object of which is to remove from your breast any suspicion that I could imagine I was bound by your Excellency's orders to expose myself to what has happened." It was a farewell message. Clinton read on: "I give you thanks for your Excellency's profuse kindness to me; and I send you the most earnest wishes for your welfare."

Clinton refused to accept reality. "God knows how much I feel for you in your present situation," he wrote back, "but I dare hope you will soon be returned from it—believe me, dear André."

Then came a sliver of hope, a secret message from the Americans: "If Sir Henry Clinton would in any way suffer General Washington to get General Arnold within his power, Major André should be immediately released."

Clinton desperately wanted to make the trade, but

knew he couldn't—if he did, no American would risk siding with the British ever again. "A deserter is never given up," he told his officers.

Though he called André "more unfortunate than criminal," Washington felt he had no choice; André must die. "Arnold or he must have been the victim," explained Hamilton, "and Arnold was out of our power." Washington approved the court's decision, and on October 1 ordered, "The execution of Major André will take place tomorrow."

André made one final appeal to Washington—he wanted to be shot, not hanged. Spies were usually hanged, but so were common criminals. It was considered more "honorable" to face a firing squad. "I trust that the request I make to your Excellency at this serious period, and which is to soften my last moments, will not be rejected," wrote André.

When he didn't hear back, André assumed the request had been granted.

John André did everything with style—he even faced his execution with flair. He spent his last night writing good-bye letters to his mother, family, and friends back home. Then he made an excellent sketch of himself sitting in prison, and presented it as a gift to his guards.

In the morning Peter Laune, who'd been André's servant in New York City, arrived with a crisp, clean uniform for his master. Laune walked into the prison, saw André, and started sobbing.

André pointed to the door, scolding, "Leave me till you can show yourself more manly!"

He had a bit of breakfast, sent to him directly from the table of George Washington. Then he shaved, tied his long hair back with a ribbon, put on his uniform and hat, and smiled to his guards.

"I am ready at any moment, gentlemen," he said.

André was led out of the stone house and down the steps. Soldiers lining the street described his face as "calm" but "pale as death." A fife and drum band played a funeral march as André walked.

He turned to an American officer and said, "Your music is excellent."

Thousands of locals and soldiers watched the march. André bowed to men he knew along the way. Witnesses say he had a weak smile on his face. A girl stepped forward and handed him a peach.

He walked past the house Washington was using for his headquarters. Washington was inside, with the shutters drawn. He had decided to deny André's request to be shot—he feared that granting it might be seen as a sign of weakness.

After a half-mile march, André spotted the gallows in a clearing ahead. "He involuntarily started backward and made a pause," said Dr. Thacher, who was walking along with André.

"Why this emotion, sir?" asked an officer.

"I am reconciled to my death," said André, "but I detest the mode of it!"

"It is unavoidable, sir."

"I have a mother and sisters who will be very much mortified."

André continued into the clearing and stopped beside a wagon beneath the gallows. Thacher watched André roll a small stone back and forth beneath his foot. His head was bowed, his checks flushed, and a sound came from his throat, said Thacher, "as if attempting to swallow."

Then André climbed onto the wagon and said, to no one in particular, "It will be but a momentary pang." He took off his hat and his long ponytail fell down his back. Colonel Scammell read the death sentence, and then added, "Major André, if you have anything to say, you can speak, for you have but a short time to live."

André looked out at the huge crowd. "I have nothing more to say, gentlemen, but this: you all bear me witness that I meet my fate as a brave man."

The hangman jumped into the wagon with André. He reached for the rope and tried to put it over André's head, but André grabbed it and, placing the loop around his own neck, drew tight the knot. He took a handkerchief from his pocket and tied it over his eyes.

There was a moment of stillness. Then the driver whipped the horses, and the wagon jolted forward. "The wagon being now removed from under him," said Thacher, "he was suspended and instantly expired."

His body swung gently at the end of the rope. "In a few minutes," said one soldier, "he hung entirely still."

Henry Clinton had held out hope—until André's servant arrived back in New York with the news. "The horrid deed is done," moaned Clinton. "Washington has committed premeditated murder!"

The entire British army was in shock. Even those who had resented André's rapid rise now mourned for the fallen hero. Arnold knew what this meant for him. When the news reached the house where he was staying, he stood up and ran out into the street. One witness described his appearance as "vastly disconcerted."

The Devil's Reward
October 3–November 14, 1780

❧

There were riots in Philadelphia. Crowds poured into the streets, barking curses and tossing firecrackers at an elaborate float featuring a large figure of Arnold—with two faces. "At the back of the general," described the *Pennsylvania Packet*, "was a figure of the Devil, dressed in black robes, shaking a purse of money at the general's left ear, and in his right hand a pitchfork, ready to drive him into hell."

"My dear sir, I have served you faithfully," said another image of Arnold on the float.

"And I'll reward you," replied the Devil.

Peggy Arnold could not go join her husband in New York—not if she was going to continue playing the innocent victim.

She asked Washington's permission to return to her family in Philadelphia. He granted it. David Franks drove their wagon through the rain. As they rattled past marching soldiers, men glared angrily up at Peggy. No one along the route would offer them lodging. Franks had to knock at door after door before finding someone who would sell him some food for Peggy.

Finally, at the New Jersey home of a Loyalist named Theodosia Prevost, Peggy received a friendly welcome. The two women walked into the sitting room and Peggy collapsed onto a couch, exhausted. According to Prevost's account, Peggy soon "became tranquillized" and began talking about her role in the plot, saying she was "disgusted with the American cause and those who had the management of public affairs." She had put on a show, convinced everyone she was blameless, but now she was "heartily tired of the theatricals she was exhibiting."

The next day Peggy continued her journey to Philadelphia. "We got here," said Franks at the end of the miserable trip. "I was very wet. Mrs. Arnold, thank God, in tolerable spirits."

Peggy climbed the stairs to her childhood room in the Shippen mansion. "She keeps to her room," said Peggy's brother-in-law, "and is almost continually on the bed. Her peace of mind seems to be entirely destroyed."

Certain his daughter was innocent, Judge Shippen erupted in venomous anti-Arnold rants. When he noticed how upset this seemed to make Peggy, he tried to keep his mouth shut.

All the while, James Reed's Pennsylvania Executive Council was searching through the papers of Benedict and Peggy Arnold. Benedict had burned all his secret correspondence, but Peggy had kept one of the letters from André, an innocent-sounding note, talking of the old days, the *Meschianza*. It proved she'd stayed in touch with André—that was enough. Shouting crowds gathered outside the Shippen home. Reed's council gave Peggy Arnold fourteen days to leave the state of Pennsylvania.

There were riots in New Haven, the city where Arnold had achieved his rise to fortune. Crackling bonfires lined the streets as fuming mobs paraded through town with a life-size Arnold effigy. The people slung a rope around the effigy's neck and hanged him from a tree. Then they set him on fire.

Washington had a theory about how the rioting was affecting Arnold. "I am mistaken if at this time Arnold is undergoing the torments of a mental hell. He wants feeling!" Washington told a friend. "He seems to have been so hackneyed in crime, so lost to all sense of honor and shame, that while his faculties still enable him to continue his sordid pursuits, there will be no time for remorse."

Washington knew Arnold well—but did Arnold really lack feeling? Or was it that he buried intense feelings beneath layers of rage and self-deception and the distraction of work? There are no firsthand accounts of what Arnold was saying in the days after his treason was discovered, let alone what he was feeling.

We do know that he stayed busy. He immediately pressured Clinton to pay him ten thousand pounds—the sum he'd asked André for in case the plot went sour. "When you consider the sacrifices I have made," he wrote, "the sum is a trifling object to the public, though of consequence to me, who has a large family that look up to me for support and protection."

Clinton arranged for Arnold to receive six thousand, plus a bit more for expenses—nearly a million dollars in today's money. Arnold used some of the money to rent a townhouse near Clinton's headquarters. Then he began bombarding Clinton with a series of written reports—plans on how to attack American forces and cities, how to put a quick end to the war. Clinton was in no mood to discuss the subject.

Not only had Arnold's plot failed, it had backfired in

his face. While Americans burned Arnold effigies, the British were not much friendlier. Officers were appalled to be suddenly outranked by this newcomer. More than that, they asked each other what kind of man betrays his country for money?

"General Arnold is a very unpopular character in the British army," one officer reported. "Officers have conceived such an aversion to him, that they unanimously refused to serve under his command."

When Peggy and baby Edward arrived in New York, Arnold picked them up and drove them through the busy streets to his rented house. They went inside and shut the door.

There were riots in Norwich. The moon lit the scene in Arnold's hometown—a gathering of thin gray graves on a small sloping hill behind a church. Engraved on two of the gravestones was the name Benedict Arnold. One was for Arnold's infant brother, the other for his father.

Mobs gathered outside the cemetery fence. They charged in, right to the two stones with the hated name. Several men stepped forward and kicked the stones over. Others lifted the slabs and smashed them to the ground.

I MUST NEVER RETURN

1780–1804

The American reaction to Arnold's betrayal went through several stages. First came shock and rage—for weeks charred Arnold effigies dangled from trees all over the country. Then people began looking at each other with suspicion. "We are all astonishment," Colonel Scammell said at the time, "each peeping at his neighbor to see if any treason was hanging about him."

Next came amazement that such a dangerous plot had come so close to working. "Had this plan succeeded," said one officer, "it must have put an end to the war." The more people thought about it, the more it seemed like an absurdly improbable series of events had saved the nation—the Cahoon brothers being too tired to row André back to the *Vulture*, the American soldiers firing on the *Vulture* without orders, the three militiamen nabbing André just moments before he was safely back to British lines. And why, when André saw the three men blocking the road, had he blurted out he was British? Imagine if he'd stuck to the plan and said he was an American on business for Arnold. If the men turned out to be Americans, they would have let him go. If they were British, they'd have delivered him, as a prisoner, to Clinton. Either way, the West Point attack would have begun hours later—with George Washington sitting in the trap.

Congress declared a day of national thanksgiving in honor of the close call. Some called it luck; others saw the hand of God. Americans pulled together, unified by the focus on a common enemy. For the first time in years, many began to believe that they could win this war after all.

One last time, Benedict Arnold had helped save the American Revolution.

That was definitely not his intention. In January 1781, wearing his new British uniform, Arnold led a raid up the James River in Virginia, slicing all the way to the capital city of Richmond. The governor, Thomas Jefferson, slipped out of town just in time to escape capture.

Several American soldiers were taken prisoner in the raid. Arnold asked one of the prisoners what he thought the Americans would do if he, Arnold, were ever captured.

"If I must answer your question, you must excuse my telling you the plain truth," said the prisoner. "If my countrymen should catch you, I believe they would first cut off that lame leg, which was wounded in the cause of freedom and virtue, and bury it with the honors of war; and afterwards hang the remainder of your body."

That was about right. Desperate to get his hands on the man who betrayed him, Washington had approved a secret plot to kidnap Arnold from his home in New York City. Arnold was to be "brought to me alive," Washington emphasized. "My aim is to make a public example of him."

A young American officer named John Champe showed up in Manhattan, telling everyone that Arnold had inspired him to desert Washington's army. His story sounded real, and he badmouthed the Americans convincingly. After signing up to fight under Arnold, Champe spent a couple of weeks studying Arnold's schedule, his habits, watching from an alley behind Arnold's townhouse. On the night the kidnapping was to take place—with Champe's accomplices waiting nearby in a rowboat—Arnold had left for the Virginia raid. It was the closest Washington came to getting Arnold, though it's hard to imagine anyone taking Arnold alive.

In September 1781, Arnold led another attack, this time on the town of New London, Connecticut, ten miles from his hometown of Norwich. His troops burned the place to the ground.

Just a month later, Washington's army and a French fleet surrounded eight thousand British soldiers at Yorktown, Virginia. The British were forced to surrender.

Benedict Arnold left the United States forever in December 1781. He and Peggy arrived in London on a cold and rainy day a month later.

Their reception, at first, was encouraging. Arnold and King George III were often seen strolling and chatting in a park near the king's palace. The king was thrilled to have found at least one person who agreed with him that the American War could still be won. But the king and Arnold were alone in this opinion. To the rest of the country, the war was an endless, expensive, unpopular disaster. In the 1783 Treaty of Paris, Britain recognized the United States as an independent nation.

Then things turned ugly. The perfect scapegoat for an

angry public, Arnold was hissed at in theaters, attacked in newspapers. Influential people ignored him. When the war ended, Arnold's sister Hannah brought his sons to Britain, and Arnold was able to get them commissioned as officers in the British army. But decent jobs in the government or military were closed to him.

He decided to start over in Canada. When he went ahead to find a house for the family, Peggy realized how alone she really was. "I am in a strange country without a creature near me that is really interested in my fate," she wrote to her father. "You will not wonder if I am unhappy."

Peggy joined Benedict in New Brunswick, where they tried to get a variety of businesses started. After six years of failure they returned to London, and failed there, too. All the while a never-ending parade of rumors and nasty newspaper articles followed Arnold—the recurring theme was the charge that lust for money had been his only motivation for changing sides. Arnold filed a long series of lawsuits, accusing enemies of destroying his reputation, ruining his business deals. He even fought a duel with a member of the House of Lords.

There's one scene that perfectly sums up Arnold's entire post-treason life. It takes place in 1793 in Falmouth,

England, during a wicked storm of wind and rain. Empty ships rocked in the port. Marooned travelers huddled in waterfront taverns.

At one of the taverns was a French nobleman, Charles Talleyrand, who was escaping the spreading violence of the French Revolution. "The innkeeper," said Talleyrand, "informed me that one of his lodgers was an American general."

Talleyrand, who was hoping to travel to the United States, asked to be introduced to the American, and the innkeeper brought him over to the man's table.

"After the mutual exchange of greetings," Talleyrand remembered, "I put to him several questions concerning his country, but, from the first, it seemed to me that my inquiries annoyed him."

Talleyrand tried again and again to get a conversation going, running through every subject he could think of. The American offered brief, dead-end responses.

Talleyrand then got to the point, explaining the real reason he'd wanted to meet the American. "I ventured to request from him some letters of introduction to his friends in America."

"No," said the man.

Talleyrand was seriously insulted. He expected some

kind of explanation. Several long seconds of silence followed.

Finally the American looked up. "I am perhaps the only American who cannot give you letters from his own country," he said. "All the relations I had there are now broken—I must never return."

Tallyrand's face rolled slowly from confusion to recognition to shock—this was Benedict Arnold.

"I must confess that he excited my pity," Talleyrand later said. To those who would condemn him for this weakness, Talleyrand offered only one excuse: "I was a witness of his agony."

Arnold's body broke down in the spring of 1801. Suffering from endless throbbing in his wounded left leg, gout in both legs, severe asthma, and gradual heart failure, Arnold stopped working and shed weight quickly.

"His legs swelled greatly," Peggy said, "and his difficulty of breathing was at times so great, particularly at night, that he could scarcely lie down." She could see that his spirit was broken; he was not going to fight anymore.

Benedict Arnold died on June 14, 1801, at the age of 60. He was buried in a small London church. "Poor

General Arnold has departed this world without notice," reported the *London Post*. Peggy Arnold died of cancer just three years later, aged 44, and was buried beside her husband.

If Arnold had died from his wounds at the Battle of Saratoga, we would think of him today as one of the all-time great American heroes. Aside from Washington, we'd say, he did more to win our Revolution than anyone. We'd celebrate his life as one of the best action stories we have—Washington never did anything half as exciting as the march to Quebec or the Battle of Valcour Island. Sure, we'd say Arnold was unstable, tormented, a loose cannon. But he'd be *our* loose cannon.

We don't say any of that, and it's all Arnold's fault. But still, it's all true.

If you visit the Saratoga battlefield, which is now a national park, you may see a very strange monument, one that perfectly symbolizes Arnold's place in the United States. It's tucked away off the main path, near tour stop number seven, the spot where Arnold led his final charge as an American general. It's a small stone sculpture of a lower left leg. No person, just a tall boot.

A plaque reads: "In memory of the most brilliant soldier of the Continental Army who was desperately wounded on this spot, the sally port of Burgoyne's Great Western Redoubt 7th October, 1777, winning for his countrymen the decisive battle of the American Revolution."

Nowhere does the monument mention the name Benedict Arnold.

BENEDICT ARNOLD

SOURCE NOTES

I've been fascinated by Benedict Arnold's story for years and have long wanted to write my own version—I'm convinced it's one of the best action/adventure tales in American history. In preparation, I compiled an absurdly large collection of books about Arnold, not to mention plays, historical prints, and other Arnold items I probably shouldn't have spent my money on.

Still hungry for more, I spent many weekends driving to the places where Benedict Arnold grew up and worked and fought and plotted. I even suggested to my wife that we use our precious vacation time on a two-week road trip along the route of Arnold's march to Quebec. And she went for it! Hiking and paddling (and mostly driving) this rugged route gave me a whole new appreciation for the incredible accomplishment of Arnold's army.

I'm guessing most readers will be slightly less obsessed with Arnold. But for anyone interested in exploring the story a bit further, the following list of books might be a good place to begin. I've included the books I used to research the life of Benedict Arnold, as well as sources with information about the other the characters and events covered in this book.

Benedict Arnold Sources

I took lots of notes from previous books about Arnold's life, battles, treason, etc. This is a list of the sources I found most helpful. There's tons of great stuff here, but I'd say the two most essential volumes are Roberts's *March to Quebec*—a massive compilation of the diaries and journals of march participants—and Van Doren's *Secret History of the American Revolution*—a clear and detailed account of the Arnold-André plot, including their complete secret correspondence.

Abbatt, William. *Crisis of the Revolution: Being the Story of Arnold and André.* New York: W. Abbatt, 1899.

Arnold, Isaac N. *The Life of Benedict Arnold.* Chicago: Jansen & McClurg, 1880.

Atwater, Edward. *History of the City of New Haven.* New York: W.W. Munsell & Co., 1887.

Caulkins, Frances Manwaring. *History of Norwich, Connecticut: From Its Possession by the Indians to the Year 1866.* Hartford, CT: Case, Lockwood and Company, 1866.

Clark, Stephen. *Following in Their Footsteps: A Travel Guide & History of the 1775 Secret Expedition to Capture Quebec.* Shapleigh, ME: Clark Books, 2003.

Desjardin, Thomas A. *Through a Howling Wilderness.* New York: St. Martin's Press, 2006.

Flexner, James Thomas, *The Traitor and the Spy: Benedict Arnold and John André.* Syracuse, NY: Syracuse University Press, 1953.

Hill, George Canning. *The Life of Benedict Arnold.* New York: A. L. Burt Company, 1884.

Martin, James Kirby. *Benedict Arnold: Revolutionary Hero*. New York: New York University Press, 1997.

Nelson, James L. *Benedict Arnold's Navy: The Ragtag Fleet that Lost the Battle of Lake Champlain but Won the American Revolution*. New York: McGraw-Hill, 2006.

Randall, Willard Sterne. *Benedict Arnold: Patriot and Traitor*. New York: Morrow, 1990.

Roberts, Kenneth, ed. *March to Quebec: Journals of the Members of Arnold's Expedition*. New York: Doubleday, Doran & Company, 1938.

Thompson, Ray. *Benedict Arnold in Philadelphia*. Fort Washington, PA: Bicentennial Press, 1975.

Todd, Charles Burr. *The Real Benedict Arnold*. New York: A. S. Barnes and Company, 1903.

Van Doren, Carl. *Secret History of the American Revolution*. New York: Viking Press, 1941.

Wallace, Willard M. *Traitorous Hero: The Life and Fortunes of Benedict Arnold*. New York: Harper & Row, 1954.

John André, Peggy Shippen, and Other Characters

John André is harder to research than Benedict Arnold—there just aren't as many good sources out there. The two most helpful to me were Flexner's *The Traitor and the Spy* and Hatch's *Major John André*. Information on Peggy Shippen was even harder to come by. The most complete source is Walker's series of articles called "Life of Margaret Shippen." I've also included some good sources on other key characters.

Chernow, Ron. *Alexander Hamilton*. New York: Penguin Press, 2004.

Flexner, James Thomas, *The Traitor and the Spy: Benedict Arnold and John André*. Syracuse, NY: Syracuse University Press, 1953.

Graham, James. *The Life of General Daniel Morgan*. New York: Derby & Jackson, 1859.

Hatch, Robert McConnell. *Major John André: A Gallant in Spy's Clothing*. Boston: Houghton Mifflin Company, 1986.

Holbrook, Stewart. *Ethan Allen*. Portland, OR: Binfords & Mort, 1958.

Leake, Isaac Q. *Memoir of the Life and Times of General John Lamb, an Officer of the Revolution*. Albany, NY: Joel Munsell, 1859.

Lossing, Benson J. *The Life and Times of Philip Schuyler, Vol. II*. New York: Sheldon & Company, 1873.

Reed, William. *The Life and Correspondence of Joseph Reed*. Philadelphia: Lindsay and Blakiston, 1847.

Sargent, Winthrop. *Life and Career of Major John André*. New York: W. Abbatt, 1902.

Tillotson, Harry Stanton. *The Beloved Spy: The Life and Loves of Major John André*. Caldwell, Idaho: The Caxton Printers, 1948.

Tillotson, Harry Stanton. *The Exquisite Exile: The Life and Fortunes of Mrs. Benedict Arnold*. Boston: Lothrop, Lee & Shepard Co., 1932.

Tower, Charlemagne. *The Marquis de La Fayette in the American Revolution. Volume II*. Philadelphia: J. B. Lippincott Company, 1895.

Walker, Lewis Burd. "Life of Margaret Shippen, Wife of Benedict
    Arnold." *Pennsylvania Magazine of History and Biography*, Vol.
    XXIV (1900), 257–267, 401–429; Vol. XXV (1901), 20–46, 145–190,
    289–302, 452–497.

Proceedings of a Board of General Officers respecting Major John André. Pub-
    lished at Philadelphia, 1780.

American Revolution Sources

During the course of my work on this book, I often found myself needing additional information about the events going on around Arnold. Here are sources
I turned to in search of details about a specific aspect of the American Revolution, a key battle, or an interesting fact about life at a particular time or place.

Barber, John W. *Historical Collections of the State of New York.* New York:
    Clark, Austin & Co., 1851.

Bell, William Clark, ed. *Naval Documents of the American Revolution, Vol-
    ume 1: 1774–1775.* Washington: U.S. Navy Department, 1964.

Bell, William Clark, ed. *Naval Documents of the American Revolution, Vol-
    umes 5 & 6: 1776.* Washington: U.S. Navy Department, 1964.

Gipson, Lawrence Henry. *Jared Ingersoll: A Study of American Loyalism in
    Relation to British Colonial Government.* New Haven: Yale Historical
    Publications, 1918.

Headly, Joel Tyler. *Chaplains and Clergy of the Revolution.* New York:
    Charles Scribner, 1864.

Ketchum, Richard M. *Saratoga: Turning Point of America's Revolutionary
    War.* New York: Henry Holt and Company, 1997.

Langguth, A. J. *Patriots: The Men Who Started the American Revolution.* New York: Touchstone, 1988.

Lossing, Benson John. *Pictorial Field Book of the American Revolution.* New York: Harper & Brothers, 1859.

Mackesy, Piers. *The War for America.* Cambridge: Harvard University Press, 1993.

McGuire, Thomas. *The Philadelphia Campaign, Volume 1: Brandywine and the Fall of Philadelphia.* Mechanicsburg, PA: Stackpole Books, 2006.

Peters, Samuel. *A General History of Connecticut.* New Haven: D. Clark and Co., 1829.

Polf, William A. *Garrison Town: The British Occupation of New York City, 1776–1783.* Albany, NY: New York State American Revolution Bicentennial Commission, 1976.

Schecter, Barnet. *The Battle for New York: The City at the Heart of the American Revolution.* New York: Walker & Co., 2002.

Smith, Justin. *Our Struggle for the Fourteenth Colony: Canada and the American Revolution.* New York: G. P. Putnam's Sons, 1907.

Stone, William. *The Campaign of Lieut. General John Burgoyne and the Expedition of Lieut. Col. Barry St. Leger.* Albany, NY: Joel Munsell, 1877.

Symonds, Craig L. and William Clipson. *A Battlefield Atlas of the American Revolution.* Baltimore: Nautical & Aviation Publishing Company of America, 1986.

Ward, Christopher. *The War of the Revolution, Volume 1.* New York: The Macmillan Company, 1952.

Wrong, George M. and H. H. Langton, eds. *Review of Historical Publications Relating to Canada.* Volume XII, 1907. Toronto: Morang & Co., 1908.

Wurtele, Fred C., ed. *Blockade of Quebec in 1775–1776 by the American Revolutionists.* Port Washington, NY: Kennikat Press, 1970.

Firsthand Accounts

I always try to let participants speak for themselves. Here's a list of books with collections of primary sources, as well as memoirs from individual participants. Lawson's *American State Trials* is an especially fascinating source, as it contains complete records of Benedict Arnold's court-martial, the trial that led to the execution of John André, *and* the treason trial of Joshua Hett Smith (who was rightfully acquitted of playing an intentional role in Arnold's plot).

Adams, John Q. "Diary of John Quincy Adams," *Proceedings of the Massachusetts Historical Society*, Second Series, Volume 16, 1902.

Allen, Ethan. *Ethan Allen's Narrative of the Capture of Ticonderoga: And of His Captivity and Treatment by the British.* Burlington, VT: Chauncey Goodrich, 1846.

Anburey, Thomas. *With Burgoyne from Quebec: An Account of the Life at Quebec and of the Famous Battle at Saratoga.* Toronto: Macmillan of Canada, 1963.

André, John. *Major André's Journal: Operations of the British Army, June 1777 to November 1778.* Tarrytown, NY: William Abbatt, 1930.

André, John. "Particulars of the Meschianza" letter written May 23, 1778. Printed in *Gentleman's Magazine*, August 1778, pp. 353–357.

Arnold, Benedict. "Benedict Arnold's Memorandum Book, from Fort Ticonderoga and Crown Point, 1775." *The Bulletin of the Fort Ticonderoga Museum.* Volume XIV, Winter 1982, pp. 71–81.

Beebe, Lewis. "Journal of a Physician on the Expedition to Canada, 1776." *Pennsylvania Magazine of History and Biography,* Volume 59 (1935), pp. 320–361.

Burgoyne, John. *A State of the Expedition from Canada.* New York: New York Times Press, 1969.

Dearborn, Henry. *Revolutionary War Journals of Henry Dearborn, 1775–1783.* Chicago: The Caxton Club, 1939.

Hibbert, Christopher. *Redcoats and Rebels: The American Revolution Through British Eyes.* New York: Avon Books, 1990.

Lawson, John. D., ed. *American State Trials: A Collection of Important and Interesting Criminal Trials.* Volume VI, St. Louis: F. H. Thomas Law Book Co., 1916.

Moore, Frank, ed. *Diary of the American Revolution: From Newspapers and Original Documents, Volume 2.* Hartford, CT: J. B. Burr, 1876.

Nichols, Francis. "Diary of Lieutenant Francis Nichols." Ed. Thomas H. Montgomery. *Pennsylvania Magazine of History and Biography,* Volume 20 (1896), pp. 504–506.

Oswald, Eleazer. "Journal Kept by Eleazer Oswald on Lake Champlain." *Bulletin of the Fort Ticonderoga Museum,* Volume XIII (1977), p. 341.

Riedesel, Friederike Charlotte Luise. *Letters and Memoirs Relating to the War of American Independence.* Chapel Hill, NC: University of North Carolina Press, 1965.

Scheer, George F. and Hugh F. Rankin. *Rebels and Redcoats: The American Revolution Through the Eyes of Those Who Fought and Lived It*. New York: Da Capo Press, 1957.

Smith, Joshua Hett. *Narrative of the Death of Major André*. New York: New York Times and Arno Press, 1969.

Sparks, Jared. *Correspondence of the American Revolution*. Cambridge: H. O. Houghton and Company, 1853.

Talleyrand, Charles Maurice. "The Memoirs of Talleyrand." *Century Illustrated Monthly Magazine*, Volume XLI (January 1891), pp. 361–376.

Thacher, James, M.D. *A Military Journal During the American Revolutionary War, From 1775 to 1783*. Boston: Cottons & Barnard, 1827.

Wells, Bayze. "Journal of Bayze Wells, May 1775–February 1777." *Collections of the Connecticut Historical Society*, Vol. VII. Hartford, CT (1899), pp. 240–297.

Wilkinson, James. *Memoirs of My Own Times*. Philadelphia: A. Small, 1816.

QUOTATION NOTES

PRANKS AND PLAYS

"daredevil": Arnold, *Life of Benedict Arnold.*
"a bright boy": Caulkins, *History of Norwich.*
"Deaths are multiplying": Randall, *Benedict Arnold.*
"For three or four days": Randall, *Benedict Arnold.*
"Your father is in a poor": Randall, *Benedict Arnold.*
"Benedict Arnold [Senior] of Norwich": Martin, *Benedict Arnold.*

MAKING OF A REBEL

"was used with the greatest humanity": Hill, *Life of Benedict Arnold.*
"I justly deserve a halter": Randall, *Benedict Arnold.*
"Near four hours after": Hill, *Life of Benedict Arnold.*
"received near forty lashes": Hill, *Life of Benedict Arnold.*
"The growing disorder": Gipson, *Jared Ingersoll.*
"a shocking, cruel and dangerous": Randall, *Benedict Arnold.*
"something below the middle height": Arnold, *Life of Benedict Arnold.*
"He was dark-skinned": Arnold, *Life of Benedict Arnold.*
"He was well formed": Arnold, *Life of Benedict Arnold.*
"The most accomplished and graceful": Arnold, *Life of Benedict Arnold.*
"I have now been in the West Indies": Randall, *Benedict Arnold.*
"I am now under the greatest": Randall, *Benedict Arnold.*
"You are a damned Yankee": Hill, *Life of Benedict Arnold.*
"I give you notice": Hill, *Life of Benedict Arnold.*
"Good God! Are the Americans": Wallace, *Traitorous Hero.*
"Bring an axe": Peters, *General History of Connecticut.*

ARNOLD'S WAR

"This is Colony property": Todd, *The Real Benedict Arnold*.
"I have certain information": Clark, *Naval Documents, Vol. 1*.
"Let every man bring as much": Smith, *Our Struggle for the Fourteenth Colony*.
"no proper orders": Arnold, *Memorandum Book*.

ACROSS THE LAKE

"What shall I do": Wallace, *Traitorous Hero*.
"I landed eighty-three men": Allen, *Capture of Fort Ticonderoga*.
"My first thought was to kill": Allen, *Capture of Fort Ticonderoga*.
"Come out of there": Martin, *Benedict Arnold*.
"I endeavored to make them hear me": Flexner, *Traitor and Spy*.
"In the name of the Great Jehovah": Smith, *Our Struggle for the Fourteenth Colony*.
"Give up your arms": Smith, *Our Struggle for the Fourteenth Colony*.
"There is here at present": Randall, *Benedict Arnold*.
"The power is now taken": Randall, *Benedict Arnold*.
"We immediately fixed her": Arnold, *Memorandum Book*.
"I have done everything:" Randall, *Benedict Arnold*.

TROUBLE AT FORT TI

"After rowing hard all night": Oswald, *Journal*.
"I surprised and took prisoners": Arnold, *Memorandum Book*.
"Just at the completion": Oswald, *Journal*.
"tossed about the flowing bowl": Allen, *Capture of Fort Ticonderoga*.
"I took the liberty": Randall, *Benedict Arnold*.
"be second in command": Wallace, *Traitorous Hero*.
"But, oh, alas": Martin, *Benedict Arnold*.

ENTER ANDRÉ

"We begin to have some notion": Flexner, *Traitor and Spy*.
"Well made, rather slender": Hatch, *Major John André*.
"He was the handsomest man:" Flexner, *Traitor and Spy*.
"I every now and then make parties": Flexner, *Traitor and Spy*.
"I had this duty yesterday": Flexner, *Traitor and Spy*.

A RISKY PROPOSITION

"An idle life": Martin, *Benedict Arnold*.
"I daresay the men would fight": Scheer and Rankin, *Rebels and Redcoats*.
"Six feet two inches in his stockings": Ward, *War of the Revolution*.
"All his features": Flexner, *Traitor and Spy*.
"It was in the gray of the morning": Headly, *Chaplains and Clergy*.
"I have detached Colonel Arnold": Desjardin, *Through a Howling Wilderness*.
"You are entrusted with a command": Arnold, *Life of Benedict Arnold*.
"They probably thought we had many": Roberts, *March to Quebec*.

TO THE DEAD RIVER

"It seemed to me that had I been thrown": Desjardin, *Through a Howling Wilderness*.
"I found the bateaux completed": Randall, *Benedict Arnold*.
"To Quebec and victory": Martin, *Benedict Arnold*.
"The men in general": Roberts, *March to Quebec*.
"Our progress under these immense": Roberts, *March to Quebec*.
"Could we have then come": Roberts, *March to Quebec*.
"Here we leave the English settlements": Roberts, *March to Quebec*.
"Our commander, Arnold": Wallace, *Traitorous Hero*.
"Arrived at the Great Carrying Place": Roberts, *March to Quebec*.
"A complete bog": Desjardin, *Through a Howling Wilderness*.

"Every step we made": Roberts, *March to Quebec*.

"Our men are fatigued": Roberts, *March to Quebec*.

"The ground was so soaked": Desjardin, *Through a Howling Wilderness*.

"The army was now much fatigued": Roberts, *March to Quebec*.

CRITICAL AND ALARMING

"Prodigious fall of rain": Roberts, *March to Quebec*.

"It was near eleven o'clock": Roberts, *March to Quebec*.

"rushing on us like a torrent": Roberts, *March to Quebec*.

"I am at this time well": Desjardin, *Through a Howling Wilderness*.

"At this critical and alarming": Roberts, *March to Quebec*.

"We could be in no worse situation": Desjardin, *Through a Howling Wilderness*.

"Our march has been attended": Roberts, *March to Quebec*.

"Pray make all possible dispatch": Roberts, *March to Quebec*.

"Our men made a general prayer": Roberts, *March to Quebec*.

"We are in an absolute danger": Desjardin, *Through a Howling Wilderness*.

"The ascent and descent of the hill": Roberts, *March to Quebec*.

"Whose heart would not have melted": Roberts, *March to Quebec*.

"We proceeded with as little knowledge": Desjardin, *Through a Howling Wilderness*.

CITY ON A CLIFF

"Happily no lives were lost": Roberts, *March to Quebec*.

"Had we been carried over": Roberts, *March to Quebec*.

"After walking a few hours": Desjardin, *Through a Howling Wilderness*.

"Every one of us shivering": Roberts, *March to Quebec*.

"Some of them were left": Desjardin, *Through a Howling Wilderness*.

"Will you leave us to perish": Roberts, *March to Quebec*.

"Warner is not here": Desjardin, *Through a Howling Wilderness*.

"She covered him with leaves": Desjardin, *Through a Howling Wilderness*.
"They ate every part of him": Roberts, *March to Quebec*.
"When we arose this morning": Desjardin, *Through a Howling Wilderness*.
"Farewell": Roberts, *March to Quebec*.
"At this sight we made a halt": Roberts, *March to Quebec*.
"A cow was immediately killed": Roberts, *March to Quebec*.
"I had the good fortune": Roberts, *March to Quebec*.
"Thus in about eight weeks": Arnold, *Life of Benedict Arnold*.
"Our clothes were torn in pieces": Randall, *Benedict Arnold*.
"The people looked upon us": Roberts, *March to Quebec*.

PRISONER OF WAR

"a barrack built for twenty-five men": Flexner, *Traitor and Spy*.
"We could see the enemy dragging cannon": Flexner, *Traitor and Spy*.
"The weather grew very cold": Flexner, *Traitor and Spy*.
"Brave men like you": Smith, *Our Struggle for the Fourteenth Colony*.
"Connecticut or such other province": Flexner, *Traitor and Spy*.

TO THE STORMING

"I propose crossing the St. Lawrence": Randall, *Benedict Arnold*.
"The night being exceeding dark": Roberts, *March to Quebec*.
"I thought we much resembled": Roberts, *March to Quebec*.
"We gave them three huzzas": Roberts, *March to Quebec*.
"I am ordered by the Excellency": Desjardin, *Through a Howling Wilderness*.
"Most of the soldiers were in constant": Roberts, *March to Quebec*.
"My detachments are as ready": Flexner, *Traitor and Spy*.
"Col. Arnold's corps": Wallace, *Traitorous Hero*.
"The attempt to storm a place": Roberts, *March to Quebec*.
"Be ready at twelve!" Randall, *Benedict Arnold*.

BATTLE FOR QUEBEC

"The storm was outrageous": Roberts, *March to Quebec*.
"We were all alarmed": Wurtele, *Blockade of Quebec*.
"Turn out! Turn out": Randall, *Benedict Arnold*.
"They sent in a number of shells": Wurtele, *Blockade of Quebec*.
"Men of New York": Arnold, *Life of Benedict Arnold*.
"It was impossible to bear up": Roberts, *March to Quebec*.
"I received a wound by a ball": Arnold, *Life of Benedict Arnold*.
"Hurry on": Randall, *Benedict Arnold*.
"Daylight had scarce made its appearance": Roberts, *March to Quebec*.
"Under these circumstances": Wallace, *Traitorous Hero*.

BLOCKADE IN THE SNOW

"For God's sake": Wallace, *Traitorous Hero*.
"Quebec is ours": Arnold, *Life of Benedict Arnold*.
"We took shelter from the fury": Roberts, *March to Quebec*.
"You are all my prisoners": Wurtele, *Blockade of Quebec*.
"Neither I, nor one in ten": Roberts, *March to Quebec*.
"Who are you": Martin, *Benedict Arnold*.
"Are you a priest": Ward, *War of the Revolution*.
"I have no thoughts of leaving": Randall, *Benedict Arnold*.
"Arnold has, to his great honor": Wallace, *Traitorous Hero*.
"God bless your honor": Wurtele, *Blockade of Quebec*.
"Colonel Arnold's march": Martin, *Benedict Arnold*.
"The merit of this gentleman": Martin, *Benedict Arnold*.
"My thanks are due": Martin, *Benedict Arnold*.
"I am greatly obliged": Wallace, *Traitorous Hero*.
"The severity of the climate": Roberts, *March to Quebec*.

ANDRÉ IN PENNSYLVANIA

"I often played marbles": Flexner, *Traitor and Spy.*
"Myself and Mr. Despard": Flexner, *Traitor and Spy.*
"We seldom have conversation": Hatch, *Major John André.*
"a very handsome young man": Flexner, *Traitor and Spy.*
"No damn Rebel should ever": Hatch, *Major John André.*
"You may thank my old mistress": Hatch, *Major John André.*
"We were every day pelted": Flexner, *Traitor and Spy.*
"perfidious dastards": Flexner, *Traitor and Spy.*
"a greasy committee": Hatch, *Major John André.*

THE LAST MAN OUT

"This is not the first or last": Sparks, *Correspondence of the American Revolution.*
"I am content to be the last": Wallace, *Traitorous Hero.*
"ordered me to follow his example": Wilkinson, *Memoirs.*
"Language cannot describe": Beebe, *Journal of a Physician.*
"The soldiers [are] either sleeping": Beebe, *Journal of a Physician.*
"General Arnold, who is perfectly skilled": Arnold, *Life of Benedict Arnold.*
"I am extremely happy": Arnold, *Life of Benedict Arnold.*

ARNOLD'S MOTLEY CREW

"We expect a bloody summer": Schecter, *Battle for New York.*
"If you want breeches": Randall, *Benedict Arnold.*
"Believe me, dear sir": Randall, *Benedict Arnold.*
"Pray hurry it up": Randall, *Benedict Arnold.*
"I cannot but think it": Martin, *Benedict Arnold.*
"The whole of the general's conduct": Wallace, *Traitorous Hero.*
"As your very nice": Randall, *Benedict Arnold.*
"I was obliged to act": Wallace, *Traitorous Hero.*

"I know no orders": Randall, *Benedict Arnold*.
"I am surprised you should": Randall, *Benedict Arnold*.
"I beg at least one hundred": Arnold, *Life of Benedict Arnold*.
"Be satisfied": Martin, *Benedict Arnold*.
"I hope to be excused": Martin, *Benedict Arnold*.
"twelve strokes on his naked buttocks": Wells, *Journal*.
"Every ship keeps half": Bell, *Naval Documents, Vol. 6*.
"Little Hal sends a kiss": Randall, *Benedict Arnold*.
"The rascals won't give": Hibbert, *Redcoats and Rebels*.

BATTLE OF VALCOUR ISLAND

"The guard boat came": Wells, *Journal*.
"We immediately prepared": Bell, *Naval Documents, Vol. 6*.
"I gave it as my opinion": Martin, *Benedict Arnold*.
"After we had in this manner": Randall, *Benedict Arnold*.
"The engagement became general": Martin, *Benedict Arnold*.
"Close to one o'clock": Bell, *Naval Documents, Vol. 6*.
"Very fierce": Nelson, *Benedict Arnold's Navy*.
"Well, Doctor, how do you like": Nelson, *Benedict Arnold's Navy*.
"The enemy fleet attacked": Nelson, *Benedict Arnold's Navy*.
"The enemy landed a large number": Bell, *Naval Documents, Vol. 6*.

THE REVOLUTION LIVES

"We rowed out clear": Nelson, *Benedict Arnold's Navy*.
"General Carleton was in a rage": Flexner, *Traitor and Spy*.
"On the whole, I think": Flexner, *Traitor and Spy*.
"The enemy came hard": Wells, *Journal*.
"The sails, rigging, and hull": Arnold, *Life of Benedict Arnold*.
"I reached this place": Randall, *Benedict Arnold*.
"The whole body of the enemy": Nelson, *Benedict Arnold's Navy*.

"I expect this stillness": Martin, *Benedict Arnold*.
"Mr. Carleton has not yet": Nelson, *Benedict Arnold's Navy*.
"The rebel fleet upon Lake Champlain": Martin, *Benedict Arnold*.
"Lake Champlain is closed": Nelson, *Benedict Arnold's Navy*.

ANDRÉ FIGHTS ON

"We are on our road": Sargent, *Life and Career of Major André*.
"spent most of his time in examining": Flexner, *Traitor and Spy*.
"I am in perfect health": Flexner, *Traitor and Spy*.
"I am in the most happy": Flexner, *Traitor and Spy*.

A QUESTION OF HONOR

"General Arnold and his troops": Bell, *Naval Documents, Vol. 6*.
"Few men ever met with so many": Randall, *Benedict Arnold*.
"I am sorry you did not get Arnold": Randall, *Benedict Arnold*.
"She puckers her mouth": Adams, *Diary*.
"I have taken the liberty": Arnold, *Life of Benedict Arnold*.
"Arnold, our evil genius": Randall, *Benedict Arnold*.
"I have been distressed": Flexner, *Traitor and Spy*.
"Surely a more active": Arnold, *Life of Benedict Arnold*.
"I beg you will not take": Martin, *Benedict Arnold*.
"I am greatly obliged": Arnold, *Life of Benedict Arnold*.
"I can no longer serve": Arnold, *Life of Benedict Arnold*.
"The point does not now admit": Arnold, *Life of Benedict Arnold*.
"I know some villain": Randall, *Benedict Arnold*.
"Miss DeBlois has positively": Randall, *Benedict Arnold*.

EXCEEDINGLY UNHAPPY

Surrender! You are my prisoner": Wallace, *Traitorous Hero*.
"the character of a devilish fighting fellow": Martin, *Benedict Arnold*.
"The ballots being taken": Martin, *Benedict Arnold*.
"What shall be done about his rank": Martin, *Benedict Arnold*.
"Money is this man's god": Randall, *Benedict Arnold*.
"It is needless to say anything": Arnold, *Life of Benedict Arnold*.
"I am exceedingly unhappy": Wallace, *Traitorous Hero*.
"as a token of their approbation": Wallace, *Traitorous Hero*.
"uninteresting and sometimes indelicate": Flexner, *Traitor and Spy*.
"I spent last evening at the war office": Wallace, *Traitorous Hero*.
"I am wearied to death": Martin, *Benedict Arnold*.
"My feelings are deeply wounded": Wallace, *Traitorous Hero*.

ARNOLD RIDES NORTH

"the most disagreeable consequences": Randall, *Benedict Arnold*.
"If General Arnold has settled": Arnold, *Life of Benedict Arnold*.
"I have thought it my duty": Arnold, *Life of Benedict Arnold*.
"Having a jolly time": von Riedesel, *Journal*.
"The only purpose it can answer": Mackesy, *War for America*.
"He means to weaken the army": Arnold, *Life of Benedict Arnold*.
"Gentlemen, I shall take the responsibility": Arnold, *Life of Benedict Arnold*.
"Nothing shall be omitted": Martin, *Benedict Arnold*.
"Nothing to be feared": Wallace, *Traitorous Hero*.

CONQUER OR DIE

"I have done all that could be done": Randall, *Benedict Arnold*.
"We ought to march out and attack": Flexner, *Traitor and Spy*.
"I have for some time past": Arnold, *Life of Benedict Arnold*.

"urged, begged, and entreated": Martin, *Benedict Arnold*.
"Arnold rushed into the thickest": Martin, *Benedict Arnold*.
"Nothing could exceed the bravery": Martin, *Benedict Arnold*.
"Both armies seemed determined": Ketchum, *Saratoga*.
"Such an explosion of fire": Ketchum, *Saratoga*.
"the hottest fire of cannon": Ketchum, *Saratoga*.
"For upwards of three hours": Moore, *Diary of the American Revolution*.
"Come on, boys": Randall, *Benedict Arnold*.
"There seemed to shoot out": Martin, *Benedict Arnold*.
"By God, I will soon": Martin, *Benedict Arnold*.
"I was instantly dispatched": Wilkinson, *Memoirs*.
"Arnold chose to give": Martin, *Benedict Arnold*.
"The enemy suffered extremely": Martin, *Benedict Arnold*.

BLOODY PIECE OF WORK

"putting to the bayonet": André, *Major André's Journal*.
"I with my own eyes": McGuire, *Philadelphia Campaign*.
"I must be vain enough": Flexner, *Traitor and Spy*.

BEYOND RECONCILIATION

"Generals Gates and Arnold": Ketchum, *Saratoga*.
"the general good behavior of the troops": Graham, *Life of Morgan*.
"Colonel Morgan's corps": Ketchum, *Saratoga*.
"Matters were altercated": Lossing, *Life and Times of Schuyler*.
"High words and gross language": Wilkinson, *Memoirs*.
"I don't know of you being": Lossing, *Life and Times of Schuyler*.
"Arnold's spirit could not brook": Lossing, *Life and Times of Schuyler*.
"Arnold retired in a rage": Wilkinson, *Memoirs*.
"the face of clay": Flexner, *Traitor and Spy*.
"I have been received": Wilkinson, *Memoirs*.

"I know not what you mean": Wilkinson, *Memoirs*.

"Where I propose to join General Washington": Flexner, *Traitor and Spy*.

"I have reason to think": Flexner, *Traitor and Spy*.

"From the best intelligence": Wilkinson, *Memoirs*.

"They were similar to a pack of hounds": Martin, *Benedict Arnold*.

"I perceived about half a mile": Wilkinson, *Memoirs*.

"I am afraid to trust you": Ketchum, *Saratoga*.

"That is nothing": Ketchum, *Saratoga*.

"rode about the camp": Wilkinson, *Memoirs*.

"No man shall keep me": Arnold, *Life of Benedict Arnold*.

"What regiment is this": Randall, *Benedict Arnold*.

"He was found on the field": Wilkinson, *Memoirs*.

"He dashed to the left": Wilkinson, *Memoirs*.

"He behaved, as I then thought": Scheer and Rankin, *Rebels and Redcoats*.

"Rush on, my brave boys": Arnold, *Life of Benedict Arnold*.

"Where are you hit": Dearborn, *Journals*.

FRACTURE BOX

"The brave General Arnold": Arnold, *Life of Benedict Arnold*.

"damned nonsense": Arnold, *Life of Benedict Arnold*.

"I watched with the celebrated": Thacher, *Military Journals*.

"The fortunes of war": Langguth, *Patriots*.

"If Old England": Ketchum, *Saratoga*.

"the greatest poltroon": Martin, *Benedict Arnold*.

"Your name, sir": Martin, *Benedict Arnold*.

"His peevishness would degrade": Flexner, *Traitor and Spy*.

"General Arnold is restored": Wallace, *Traitorous Hero*.

"May I venture to ask": Arnold, *Life of Benedict Arnold*.

"As soon as your situation": Arnold, *Life of Benedict Arnold*.

PEGGY SHIPPEN

"I believe I shall be": Flexner, *Traitor and Spy*.
"a poor actor": Randall, *Benedict Arnold*.
"We were all in love": Randall, *Benedict Arnold*.
"Nobody in America": Walker, *Life of Margaret Shippen*.
"The country will be laid waste": Flexner, *Traitor and Spy*.
"*Sir William, he, snug*": Hibbert, *Redcoats and Rebels*.

BACK TO PHILADELPHIA

"Twenty times I have taken": Tillotson, *Exquisite Exile*.
"Pardon me, dear Betsy": Randall, *Benedict Arnold*.
"The music": Flexner, *Traitor and Spy*.
"selected from the foremost in youth": Randall, *Benedict Arnold*.
"Knights of the Blended Rose" André, *Particulars of the Meschianza*.
"the most splendid entertainment": Randall, *Benedict Arnold*.
"We never had, and perhaps": Flexner, *Traitor and Spy*.
"greatly resembled a fair": Flexner, *Traitor and Spy*.
"Captain André also took": Sargent, *Life of Major André*.
"*If at the close of war*": Flexner, *Traitor and Spy*.

CUPID'S WOUND

"Adopt such measures": Randall, *Benedict Arnold*.
"to remove property": Lawson, *State Trials*.
"I must tell you that Cupid": Randall, *Benedict Arnold*.
"There can be no doubt": Randall, *Benedict Arnold*.
"Will you not think it extraordinary": Wallace, *Traitorous Hero*.
"It is enough for me": Wallace, *Traitorous Hero*.
"If things proceed in the same train": Reed, *Life and Correspondence*.

"There are many persons": Van Doren, *Secret History*.
"Arnold has rendered himself": Flexner, *Traitor and Spy*.

ARNOLD UNDER ATTACK

"Twenty times I have taken": Tillotson, *Exquisite Exile*.
"Major Franks's orders were": Lawson, *State Trials*.
"I thought I had ordered you": Lawson, *State Trials*.
"The respect due to a citizen": Flexner, *Traitor and Spy*.
"If the declaration": Wallace, *Traitorous Hero*.
"Poor Peggy, how I pity her": Thompson, *Arnold in Philadelphia*.
"They say she intends to surrender": Wallace, *Traitorous Hero*.
"some gentleman of high rank": Randall, *Benedict Arnold*.
"This mode of attacking": Randall, *Benedict Arnold*.
"When I meet your carriage": Van Doren, *Secret History*.
"I shall only say": Van Doren, *Secret History*.
"the indignity offered us": Van Doren, *Secret History*.
"Animosities run high": Wallace, *Traitorous Hero*.
"abusive misrepresentations": Van Doren, *Secret History*.
"Never did I so long to see": Flexner, *Traitor and Spy*.

ANDRÉ IN NEW YORK

"Well, well, my dear child": Tillotson, *Beloved Spy*.
"Why, that's Major André": Tillotson, *Beloved Spy*.
"a cringing, insidious sycophant": Randall, *Benedict Arnold*.

DELAY WORSE THAN DEATH

"served up as a constant dish": Wallace, *Traitorous Hero*.
"I think the world are running mad": Walker, *Life of Margaret Shippen*.

QUOTATION NOTES

"I find myself under a necessity": Flexner, *Traitor and Spy*.
"If your Excellency thinks me": Randall, *Benedict Arnold*.

EVERYTHING AT STAKE

"General Arnold communicated": Van Doren, *Secret History*.
"I have received your favor": Flexner, *Traitor and Spy*.
"Should the abilities and zeal": Van Doren, *Secret History*.
"The lady might write to me": Van Doren, *Secret History*.
"Sir Henry may depend": Van Doren, *Secret History*.
"He can concur with you in almost any": Van Doren, *Secret History*.
"He self-invited some civilities": Reed, *Life and Correspondence*.

THE PRICE OF WEST POINT

"He expects to have your promise": Van Doren, *Secret History*.
"Permit me to prescribe": Van Doren, *Secret History*.
"A mob of lawless ruffians": Thompson, *Arnold in Philadelphia*.
"It is disagreeable to be accused": Lawson, *State Trials*.
"The court sentences him": Lawson, *State Trials*.
"I ought to receive a reprimand": Wallace, *Traitorous Hero*.
"Even the shadow of a fault": Lossing, *Pictorial Field Book*.
"the key to America": Randall, *Benedict Arnold*.
"If I point out a plan": Van Doren, *Secret History*.
"Should we through your means": Van Doren, *Secret History*.

ATTACKING FORT ARNOLD

"asked me if I had thought of anything": Randall, *Benedict Arnold*.
"He appeared to be quite fallen": Flexner, *Traitor and Spy*.
"This information affected her": Walker, *Life of Margaret Shippen*.

"Major General Arnold will take": Walker; *Life of Margaret Shippen*.
"General Arnold surrendering himself": Wallace, *Traitorous Hero*.
"Good fortune still follows": Hatch, *Major André*.
"His head appeared to me": Flexner, *Traitor and Spy*.
"It is surrounded on two sides": Flexner, *Traitor and Spy*.
"You must by all means": Walker; *Life of Margaret Shippen*.
"Every idea you can form": Flexner, *Traitor and Spy*.
"An unfortunate piece of business": Van Doren, *Secret History*.
"I have almost ceased": Arnold, *Life of Benedict Arnold*.
"The mass of the people": Randall, *Benedict Arnold*.
"It was certainly necessary": Van Doren, *Secret History*.
"I will send a person": Wallace, *Traitorous Hero*.
"You will keep this to yourself": Randall, *Benedict Arnold*.

THE FLOATING *VULTURE*

"To Major André": Tillotson, *Beloved Spy*.
"I do feel rather serious": Tillotson, *Beloved Spy*.
"Mr. Smith spoke to me": Van Doren, *Secret History*.
"I was sorry I was wanted": Van Doren, *Secret History*.
"The night was serene": Smith, *Narrative of the Death*.
"Very little conversation passed": Smith, *Narrative of the Death*.
"I went as directed": Smith, *Narrative of the Death*.
"I told him I was fatigued": Van Doren, *Secret History*.
"He seemed shy, and desirous": Smith, *Narrative of the Death*.
"Firing at a ship": Tillotson, *Beloved Spy*.
"Many others struck the sails": Van Doren, *Secret History*.
"He cast an anxious look": Smith, *Narrative of the Death*.

NO-MAN'S LAND

"made me put the papers": Sargent, *Life of Major André*.
"Permit Mr. John Anderson": Wallace, *Traitorous Hero*.
"I was induced to put": Sargent, *Life of Major André*.
"At the decline of the sun": Flexner, *Traitor and Spy*.
"Mr. Anderson seemed very": Smith, *Narrative of the Death*.
"I told him who I was": Smith, *Narrative of the Death*.
"No one slept safely in his bed": Smith, *Narrative of the Death*.
"He appeared in the morning": Smith, *Narrative of the Death*.
"Here comes a gentleman": Abbatt, *Crisis of the Revolution*.

PAPERS OF A DANGEROUS TENDENCY

"My lads, I hope you belong": Abbatt, *Crisis of the Revolution*.
"Get down. We're Americans": Randall, *Benedict Arnold*.
"Had he pulled out General": Lawson, *State Trials*.
"Gentlemen, you had best": Lossing, *Pictorial Field Book*.
"We found his stockings": Abbatt, *Crisis of the Revolution*.
"This is a spy": Hatch, *Major John André*.
"Any sum you want": Abbatt, *Crisis of the Revolution*.
"You could read in his face": Abbatt, *Crisis of the Revolution*.
"I forgot the olive oil": Van Doren, *Secret History*.
"It is with the greatest concern": Flexner, *Traitor and Spy*.
"General, you are going": Barber, *Historical Collections*.
"I observed in him an embarrassment": Flexner, *Traitor and Spy*.
"He had a passport signed": Flexner, *Traitor and Spy*.
"His Excellency is nigh at hand": Flexner, *Traitor and Spy*.
"in great confusion": Van Doren, *Secret History*.

A SCENE TOO SHOCKING

"Is not General Arnold here": Leake, *Life of General Lamb*.
"The impropriety of his conduct": Randall, *Benedict Arnold*.
"I heard a shriek": Van Doren, *Secret History*.
"Arnold has betrayed me": Randall, *Benedict Arnold*.
"A search was made": Tower, *Marquis de Lafayette*.
"I request you will be as vigilant": Tillotson, *Beloved Spy*.
"Transactions of a most": Tillotson, *Beloved Spy*.
"The General assured her": Van Doren, *Secret History*.
"It was the most affecting scene": Chernow, *Alexander Hamilton*.
"The unhappy Mrs. Arnold": Tower, *Marquis de Lafayette*.
"The door of the room wherein": Smith, *Narrative of the Death*.
"Sir, do you know": Smith, *Narrative of the Death*.
"Never was there a more": Flexner, *Traitor and Spy*.

READY AT ANY MOMENT

"I have ever acted from a principle": Van Doren, *Secret History*.
"The general has escaped": Flexner, *Traitor and Spy*.
"Do you recall his fate": Tillotson, *Beloved Spy*.
"It is not possible to save him": Wallace, *Traitorous Hero*.
"He behaved with so much frankness": Tower, *Marquis de Lafayette*.
"Major André, Adjutant General": Tillotson, *Beloved Spy*.
"I foresee my fate": Flexner, *Traitor and Spy*.
"He could scare finish": Chernow, *Alexander Hamilton*.
"I have obtained General Washington's": Flexner, *Traitor and Spy*.
"God knows how much I feel": Hatch, *Major John André*.
"A deserter is never given up": Hatch, *Major John André*.
"more unfortunate than criminal": Wallace, *Traitorous Hero*.
"Arnold or he must have been": Flexner, *Traitor and Spy*.
"The execution of Major André": Flexner, *Traitor and Spy*.
"I trust that the request": Hatch, *Major John André*.

"Leave me till you can show": Flexner, *Traitor and Spy.*
"I am ready at any moment": Thacher, *Military Journal.*
"Your music is excellent": Flexner, *Traitor and Spy.*
"Why this emotion, sir": Thacher, *Military Journal.*
"It will be but a momentary pang": Thacher, *Military Journal.*
"Major André, if you have anything": Hatch, *Major John André.*
"I have nothing more to say": Flexner, *Traitor and Spy.*
"The wagon being now removed": Thacher, *Military Journal.*
"The horrid deed is done": Randall, *Benedict Arnold.*
"vastly disconcerted": Flexner, *Traitor and Spy.*

THE DEVIL'S REWARD

"At the back of the general": Todd, *The Real Benedict Arnold.*
"disgusted with the American cause": Van Doren, *Secret History.*
"I was very wet": Randall, *Benedict Arnold.*
"She keeps to her room": Van Doren, *Secret History.*
"I am mistaken if at this time": Randall, *Benedict Arnold.*
"When you consider the sacrifices": Van Doren, *Secret History.*
"General Arnold is a very unpopular": Randall, *Benedict Arnold.*

I MUST NEVER RETURN

"We are all astonishment": Flexner, *Traitor and Spy.*
"Had this plan succeeded": Randall, *Benedict Arnold.*
"If I must answer your question": Hibbert, *Redcoats and Rebels.*
"My aim is to make a public example": Randall, *Benedict Arnold.*
"I am in a strange country": Walker, *Life of Margaret Shippen.*
"The innkeeper informed me": Talleyrand, *Memoirs.*
"I am perhaps the only American": Talleyrand, *Memoirs.*
"His legs swelled greatly": Walker, *Life of Margaret Shippen.*
"Poor General Arnold has departed": Randall, *Benedict Arnold.*
"In memory of the most brilliant": Martin, *Benedict Arnold.*

INDEX

D

E

F

G

H

STEVE SHEINKIN

What did you want to be when you grew up?
At first, a baseball player, but then I real-ized baseball players have to be really good at baseball. Writing was always on my mind too. As a kid, my brother and I would write comedy sketches and draw comics, and I think that got me into the idea of being a writer.

What's your most embarrassing childhood memory?
When my father dropped me off for the first day of first grade, I broke out crying in front of the whole class and said, "I'm not staying!" And then when my father insisted, I said, still weep-ing, "Fine, I'll stay, but I won't do any work!" Kids in that school never let me forget that scene.

As a young person, who did you look up to most?
Had to be my father, who was a doctor, a pilot, an author, and an all-around cool guy. He just did his thing and didn't seem to care what anyone thought about him, which I found amazing.

What was your favorite thing about school?
I loved hearing stories, and I didn't care much if they were fiction or history or science or what. I always liked writing and illustrating my own versions of stories.

What was your least favorite thing about school?
Spelling and anything to do with grammar. I was just looking back at some old report cards, and a teacher was politely explaining that "language skills don't come as easily to Stephen as to many others."

What were your hobbies as a kid?
As a kid, I loved playing sports with my friends. It didn't matter that we weren't that great; we had fun inventing plays and situations and characters and weaving them into our games. And I loved running around outside and getting dirty.

What was your first job, and what was your "worst" job?
In high school I cut lawns for a few families in our neighborhood. I could get as much as $15 for a few hours of work, which seemed like a fortune. My worst jobs were all restaurant related: busboy, host, bartender. I was fired from two restaurants, both times for not being friendly enough with the customers. I wasn't rude, exactly. I just don't like talking that much.

What book is on your nightstand now?
Conquistador, about the Spanish and the Aztecs and their epic showdown in the 1500s, plus lots of books about art forgery and art theft, subjects I find fascinating.

Where do you write your books?
I have an office at home, but I mostly work at my local library and coffee shops. People tell me they'd love to work at home because then they could sit around in their pajamas. But I don't really like pajamas.

How did you first become interested in Benedict Arnold?
I got interested in Arnold while writing an earlier book called *King George: What Was His Problem?* I put in a few pages of Arnold action, but I knew I had to do more with the story.

What is your favorite part of research?
I love reading, but the best part is when I get to travel and see historical sites with my own eyes. Luckily for me, Arnold lived and fought mainly in the northeast United States, where I live, so I was able to take a lot of Benedict Arnold road trips.

What was the coolest thing you discovered during your research?
I was fascinated by how differently Arnold is viewed in different places. In his hometown of Norwich, Connecticut, they hardly admit he exists. I think this is a big mistake on their part, because people are interested in his story and would like to see sites related to his life. In contrast, once you get to Canada, the attitude is totally different. I saw everything from rivers to restaurants to trash cans named after Arnold!

Was there anything you thought was fascinating but couldn't include in the book?

I always end up cutting stories I love just because they don't fit, or they mess up the flow of the action. Right before the Americans attack Fort Ticonderoga at the very start of the Revolutionary War, there is this great scene where a bunch of Green Mountain Boys are searching for boats and find something unexpected. My editor and I ended up cutting it because we were worried about slowing down the action. Here's the never-before-seen scene:

> Allen's boat-stealing boys were behind schedule. They'd made it to the estate of Loyalist Philip Skeene, where they found a thirty-three-foot boat tied up at the waterfront. But, realizing the place was completely abandoned,

they decided to break into Skeene's mansion, see if there was anything worth swiping.

Inside the house the men saw what looked like a lead coffin, dimly outlined by the light of the moon. Lifting the lid, they found another coffin, a fancy wooden one. Turns out Philip Skeene had married a woman from a very rich family, and the family agreed to continue sending the wife a hefty annual payment "whilst she is above ground"— meaning while she was alive, obviously. But when his wife died, Skeene devised a different interpretation, sealing the woman inside this double coffin, which locked in the stench of her rotting body. Mr. Skeene was able to report to the in-laws that his wife was very much "above ground," and the family money kept rolling in.

Allen's boys knew none of this—just that there was a corpse in the parlor. They found the scene pretty creepy, though they overcame their fears long enough to grab several bottles of what Skeene would later describe as his "choice liquors." Then they ran down to the water, jumped in the boat, and passed the bottles around as they rowed out into the lake.

Do you relate to Benedict in any way?
I can relate to his frustration with politics and politicians. He just didn't have the patience to play the game, which I can understand.

How long was your research period for *The Notorious Benedict Arnold*?
I spent years reading about Arnold, but much of that was before I officially started writing the book—that is, before anyone offered to pay me to do it. Once I had a publishing deal, I

spent about a year and a half researching and writing and editing.

Which part of the process do you prefer, writing or researching? Why?
Researching is way more fun. Like so many writers I talk to, I don't really like writing. I mean, I don't like staring at a blank piece of paper or computer screen and trying to put what's in my mind into words. It takes a lot of discipline and willpower to get started.

What do you do on a rainy day?
Same as most sunny days: I sit somewhere quiet and read and write. At a school visit once, when I described my job, a student said, "So, um, you do homework for a living?" I'd never thought of it like that, and I don't like to, but I guess there's something to it. Except I get to make up my own assignments.

What's your idea of fun?
Doing stuff outdoors, like biking and kayaking. Browsing the nonfiction sections of bookstores and libraries in search of great stories. And eating.

What was your favorite book when you were a kid? Do you have a favorite book now?
Hands down, it was the *Mutiny on the Bounty* trilogy—historical novels about a real-life mutiny on a British ship in the 1700s and the incredible aftermath. These days I'm most into true adventure/survival stories, like Ernest Shackleton's *South*, about being stranded in Antarctica, or Nathaniel Philbrick's *In the Heart of the Sea*, about a whaling ship that was rammed and sunk by a whale, and the terrible ordeal of the survivors.

If you were stranded on a desert island, who would you want for company?

My wife and two kids. I know we'd drive each other crazy, and the kids would fight over coconuts and stuff, but we'd have fun anyway.

If you could travel anywhere in the world, where would you go and what would you do?

I just finished working on a book called *Bomb*, about the race to make the first atomic bomb during World War II. There are lots of action scenes set in Norway, and I wasn't able to travel there to see the setting for myself. So I'm dying to go there and travel around the remote mountains and fjords.

If you could travel in time, where would you go and what would you do?

I couldn't pass up the chance to meet Benedict Arnold, George Washington, and all the other big shots of that era. It's so hard to get to know them through history books alone. Then I'd come back to the present and tell everyone what those guys were *really* like.

What's the best advice you have ever received about writing?

First picture what you're trying to say as if it's a movie. Then write what you see as simply and clearly as you can.

What advice do you wish someone had given you when you were younger?

That you can have many careers, one after the other. The important thing is to pick something and do it all-out. Then, if you want to, try something new.

Do you ever get writer's block? What do you do to get back on track?
Yes, sometimes. Even with nonfiction, you can get stuck trying to figure out how to explain something, or what order to put scenes in. It always helps to step away from the problem and work on something else. But ultimately, sadly, the only solution for me is to work harder.

What do you want readers to remember about your books?
I hope they remember the stories and characters, and I hope they're inspired to find out more about whatever part of the story interests them the most. But mostly I just want my books to be entertaining.

What would you do if you ever stopped writing?
I'd say teaching, but I don't think I'm outgoing enough. I think maybe I'd become a fish farmer. Don't know the first thing about it, but I'm interested.

What should people know about you?
In addition to history books, I also write and draw comics, and I'm working on some ideas for novels, too. Back in my twenties, I made a movie with my brother, a political comedy called *A More Perfect Union*. It showed at a few festivals and got some nice reviews, but then it sort of disappeared. Great learning experience, though.

What do you wish you could do better?
With every book I've ever done, I have moments where I lose confidence and think the whole thing is going to stink. It would be great if this didn't happen every time, but I just can't seem to avoid it.

What do you like best about yourself?
I'm pretty good at not giving up (see above question).

What do you consider to be your greatest accomplishment?
Being a father, which is way harder than being a writer.

What would your readers be most surprised to learn about you?
I don't actually enjoy writing. I love the process of finding stories and hunting down all the little details. It's sort of like detective work. And I love figuring out how to put all the pieces of the story together. But then comes the hard part—writing actual sentences. It's always okay once I get started, but that sometimes takes a while.

In December of 1938, a chemist in a German laboratory discovered how to split Uranium atoms in two. That shocking innovation launched a scientific race that spanned three continents. This is the story of the plotting, risk taking, deceit, and genius that created the world's most formidable weapon.

STEVE SHEINKIN

BOMB

THE RACE TO BUILD —AND STEAL— THE WORLD'S MOST DANGEROUS WEAPON

Read more to discover the story of the atomic bomb in

BOMB.

PROLOGUE: MAY 22, 1950

HE HAD A FEW MORE MINUTES to destroy seventeen years of evidence.

Still in pajamas, Harry Gold raced around his cluttered bedroom, pulling out desk drawers, tossing boxes out of the closet, and yanking books from the shelves. He was horrified. Everywhere he looked were incriminating papers—a plane ticket stub, a secret report, a letter from a fellow spy.

Gold ripped the papers to shreds, carried two fistfuls to the bathroom, shoved them into the toilet, and flushed. Then he ran back to his bedroom, grabbed the rest of the pile, and stumbled on slippers down the stairs to the cellar, where he pushed the stuff to the bottom of an overflowing garbage can.

The doorbell rang.

Gold walked to the door. He took a few deep breaths, trying to slow his heartbeat, then opened the door and saw the men he expected: Federal Bureau of Investigation agents Scott Miller and Richard Brennan. They'd been questioning Gold for days, showing him pictures of known spies, demanding information about his connection to these people. Gold had admitted nothing, insisting he was what he appeared to be: a simple, hardworking chemist who lived with his father and brother, and had never been far from his

Philadelphia home. Unconvinced, the FBI agents had come to search his house.

Gold led the way to his room. Agent Miller sat down at Gold's desk and started opening drawers, sifting through paper piles. Brennan went to work on the sagging bookshelves, packed tight with math and science volumes, and stacks of paperback novels.

Brennan flipped through a paperback, stopping to inspect something stamped on the inside cover: the name of a department store in Rochester, New York.

"What's this?" he asked Gold, holding up the open book.

"Oh, I don't know," Gold said, "must have picked it up on a used book counter somewhere. Lord knows where."

Then, from a desk drawer, Miller pulled a train schedule for the Washington–Philadelphia–New York–Boston passenger line. Another clue that Gold wasn't the homebody he'd described.

"What's this, Harry?" Miller asked.

"Goodness knows," Gold said, shrugging. "I probably picked it up when I went to New York." *This is bad*, he said to himself. *Bad, but not terrible.*

Then came the body blow.

Gold watched Brennan slide a thick, tattered copy of *Principles of Chemical Engineering* from the shelf. Nausea swelled Gold's throat as he saw a light brown, folded street map drop to the floor. To Gold, the map seemed to scream its title in the silent room: "New Mexico, Land of Enchantment."

Oh God, he thought.

"So you were never west of the Mississippi," said Brennan, bending down to lift the map. He opened it and saw, at the spot in Santa Fe where the Castillo Street Bridge crosses the Santa Fe River, an *X* marked in ink.

"How about this, Harry?" demanded Brennan.

Miller spun from the desk, stood, and watched Gold.

Gold needed to speak quickly, needed to offer an explanation. But he froze.

"Give me a minute," he managed, falling heavily into his desk chair.

Brennan offered him a cigarette, which he took. Brennan lit it, and Gold drew deeply.

"A torrent of thoughts poured through my mind," Gold later said of this moment. The map could easily be explained—he'd just say he loved Western stories, which was true, and that, out of curiosity, he'd sent to a Santa Fe museum for the map. Surely they didn't keep records of such requests; no one could prove he was lying.

But then he thought about what would happen if he continued claiming innocence: "My family, people with whom I worked, and my friends whom I knew, my lifetime friends—they would all rally around me. And how horrible would be their disappointment, and the letdown, when finally it was shown who I really was."

Harry Gold had been living a double life for seventeen years. Overwhelmed by exhaustion, he turned to the FBI agents. They were still waiting for an answer.

"Yes, I am the man," Gold said.

He slumped a little lower in his chair.

"There is a great deal more to this story. It goes way back," he said. "I would like to tell it all."